Strategic Studies Institute
and
U.S. Army War College Press

RUSSIA'S COUNTERINSURGENCY IN NORTH CAUCASUS: PERFORMANCE AND CONSEQUENCES

The Strategic Threat of Religious Extremism and Moscow's Response

Ariel Cohen

March 2014

*****

Comments pertaining to this report are invited and should be forwarded to: Director, Strategic Studies Institute and U.S. Army War College Press, U.S. Army War College, 47 Ashburn Drive, Carlisle, PA 17013-5010.

*****

This manuscript was funded by the U.S. Army War College External Research Associates Program. Information on this program is available on our website, *www.StrategicStudies Institute.army.mil*, at the Opportunities tab.

*****

*****

The Strategic Studies Institute and U.S. Army War College Press publishes a monthly email newsletter to update the national security community on the research of our analysts, recent and forthcoming publications, and upcoming conferences sponsored by the Institute. Each newsletter also provides a strategic commentary by one of our research analysts. If you are interested in receiving this newsletter, please subscribe on the SSI website at *www.StrategicStudiesInstitute.army.mil/newsletter*.

FOREWORD

The North Caucasus has been a source of instability for Russia ever since the Russian Empire brought the region under its control in the course of the late-18th and the first half of the 19th centuries. General Alexei Yermolov, a top Russian commander in North Caucasus, used inhumanely harsh methods to conquer the region and retain it under the Romanov crown's control. Hundreds of thousands were ethnically cleansed, and many civilians murdered.

In the Russian Civil War (1918-21), which took place right after World War I, the North Caucasus became a victim of both the tsarist White Army and the communist Red Army, who plundered the region and refused to give its peoples the rights they hoped to regain after the war was over. A little over 2 decades after that, the North Caucasus nations faced merciless deportations as a result of imaginary crimes they allegedly committed against the Soviet Union during World War II. Hundreds of thousands of Chechens and Ingush were ethnically cleansed and forcibly relocated to Kazakhstan's frozen steppes, Central Asian deserts, and elsewhere. In the 1990s, Chechen demands for independence led to two devastating wars, which resulted in tens of thousands of casualties, destroyed cities and villages, and hundreds of thousands of refugees.

Today, the region reminds one of a simmering cauldron, and the issues that caused so much violence in the past have not been resolved. Russia has basically granted Chechnya a de facto independence, complemented by huge federal monetary subsidies, in order to prevent it from trying to claim de jure independence again. This strategy has so far been successful. However, the fragile stability in Chechnya is now based on the depth of the Kremlin's pockets; the whims of the current Chechen leader, Ramzan Kadyrov; and on appeasing the local population with federal money. How long this bargain between the Kremlin, Kadyrov, and the Chechen people will last remains to be seen.

Ethnic Russians, tired of the cronyism and rigidity of their public institutions, watch with jealousy how much money the North Caucasian "aliens" keep getting from the federal budget. The nationalists march under the slogan "Enough feeding the Caucasus," creating a deep fissure between citizens of the same country. Meanwhile, the nations of the North Caucasus lack a system that would allow people to freely pursue their personal aspirations. Due to poverty, high unemployment, and higher birth rates in the North Caucasus than in the rest of Russia, the problem is likely to get worse.

If the situation gets out of control, the consequences are hard to predict. The North Caucasus shares borders with similarly unstable South Caucasus, and has close ties to the Middle East and Afghanistan, with ramifications both in terms of terrorism and drug trafficking. Therefore, it is a shared interest of the United States, Europe, and Russia to make sure that the North Caucasus remains stable and does not become a breeding ground for terrorist activity both within Russia and abroad.

Douglas C. Lovelace

DOUGLAS C. LOVELACE, JR.
Director
Strategic Studies Institute and
    U.S. Army War College Press

ABOUT THE AUTHOR

Ariel Cohen is a recognized authority on international security and energy policy, and the rule of law. He is a leading expert in Russia/Eurasia, Eastern Europe, and the Middle East, and serves as a Senior Research Fellow in Russian and Eurasian Studies and International Energy Policy at The Heritage Foundation. Dr. Cohen frequently testifies before committees of the U.S. Congress, including the Senate and House Foreign Relations Committees, the House Armed Services Committee, the House Judiciary Committee, and the Helsinki Commission. Dr. Cohen regularly lectures at the request of U.S. Government institutions: the U.S. Department of State, the Joint Chiefs of Staff, the Training and Doctrine and Special Forces Commands of the U.S. armed services, the Central Intelligence Agency, and the Defense Intelligence Agency. He also conducts White House briefings and directs high-level conferences on international security, energy, the rule of law, crime and corruption, and a variety of other issues. Dr. Cohen consults for Fortune 500 companies and international law firms. He served as a Senior Consultant for Burson Marsteller's Emerging Markets practice, a global public affairs firm, and for Emerging Markets Communications, a boutique strategic communications consultancy. He has prepared expert testimonies and/or testified in high-profile cases tried by leading Washington law firms; and wrote expert opinions for investors who are involved in multi-billion dollar suits against illegal expropriations in the countries of Eastern Europe and Eurasia. Dr. Cohen was a Policy Adviser with the National Institute for Public Policy's Center for Deterrence Analysis and has consulted for U.S. Agency for International Development, the World Bank, the Pentagon, the U.S. Senate, and Radio Liberty-Radio Free Europe. Dr. Cohen is a member of the Editorial Board of *Central Asia and the Caucasus* (Stockholm) and is on the Board of Advisors of the Institute for Analysis of Global Security, Endowment for Middle East Truth, and Jerusalem Center for Public Affairs. He is also a member of the Council of Foreign Relations, the International Institute for Strategic Studies (London), and the American Council on Germany. Dr. Cohen has published six books and monographs, 30 book chapters, and over 500 articles in professional and popular media. He appeared on CNN, NBC, CBS, FOX, C-SPAN, BBC-TV, Al Jazeera English, and all Russian and Ukrainian national TV networks. He was a commentator on a Voice of America weekly radio and TV show for 8 years. Currently, he is a Contributing Editor to *The National Interest* and a blogger for the Voice of America. For 8 years, he wrote commentary columns for *United Press International, Middle East Times*, and has extensively written as a guest columnist for *The New York Times, International Herald Tribune, Christian Science Monitor, The Washington Post, The Wall Street Journal, The Washington Times, EurasiaNet*, and *National Review Online*. In Europe, his analyses have appeared in *Kommersant; Izvestiya; Hurriyet;* the popular Russian website, *Ezhenedelny Zhurnal;* and many others.

SUMMARY

This monograph examines the underlying issues behind the continuing low-level Islamist insurgency movement in the Russian North Caucasus. It begins by analyzing the history of relations between the Russian and the North Caucasus nations, focusing specifically on the process of subjugating the region by the Russian Empire. Since the 18th century, Russia has used brutal force to expand territorially to the Caucasus. The mistreatment of the North Caucasus continued after World War I and especially during and after World War II, when entire North Caucasus nations faced persecution and forcible deportations to remote parts of the Soviet Union—in which up to 30 percent of the exiles perished. Thus, the Russians planted the seeds of resentment and hatred toward them that persist to the present time.

These tragic events lie at the heart of the grudges the Chechens, the Ingush, the Circassians, and other North Caucasus nations feel against the Russians. Right after the fall of communism in Eastern Europe and the breakup of the Soviet Union, these grudges came to the surface. Chechnya tried to break free from what the Chechens considered occupation of their lands by the infidel Russians. Its attempt was suppressed in two wars so as to preserve the territorial integrity of the Russian Federation.

The First Chechen War lasted from 1994 to 1996 and revealed a startling lack of combat readiness of the Russian military. However, Russia learned military lessons from the botched 1994-96 campaign and handily won the Second Chechen War of 1999-2000. Both Chechen wars resulted in tens of thousands of casualties (both military and civilian) and hundreds of thousands of refugees.

After the wars, Moscow used vast funds to rebuild Chechnya materially, but the grudges of the people have remained. Stability in Chechnya now depends on the current Kremlin-appointed Chechen president, Ramzan Kadyrov. Moscow continues to allocate significant federal funds for Chechnya and turns a blind eye to local corrupt practices, which are often a direct violation of the Russian federal law.

Without immediate, thorough, and concerted international action, the challenges that the North Caucasus presents to the world may grow into major problems. The United States must engage its allies and work with Russia to strengthen its border security, invigorate law enforcement and counterterrorist cooperation with national and international agencies, counter Islamist propaganda, improve intelligence capabilities, and appeal for international cooperation to eliminate the financial support of terrorism that helps North Caucasus militant groups flourish.

RUSSIA'S COUNTERINSURGENCY IN NORTH CAUCASUS: PERFORMANCE AND CONSEQUENCES

The Strategic Threat of Religious Extremism and Moscow's Response

The Russian North Caucasus, including the Republics of Chechnya, Dagestan, and Ingushetia, is transforming into a dangerous, ungovernable area in which global Islamic terrorism thrives. After conventional military operations of 1994-96 and 1999-2000 ended, the region has become a nexus for spreading global jihadi violence, as the attack on the Boston Marathon by the Tsarnaev brothers demonstrated. Al-Qaeda's Ayman al-Zawahiri called the North Caucasus "one of three primary fronts in the war against the West"[1] — something many in the West, including United States, have not noticed. This is a threat not just to Russia, but also to Europe — and global stability. While Russia and North Caucasian peoples had endured war, violence, and upheaval since the 1700s, the region's unprecedented emergence as a center of global Islamic terrorism is a recent phenomenon that started in the mid-1990s.

Terrorism as a tactic among North Caucasus-based Islamist groups is a recent trend but has swiftly catapulted into the primary form of violence against Russia and the global Salafi-jihadi movement's international targets. The radical North Caucasus groups include Jamaat Shariat (the Dagestani Front of the Caucasus Emirate's Armed Forces), Yarmuk Jamaat (the Armed Forces of the United Vilayat [Province] of Kabarda-Balkaria-Karachai), Ingush Jamaat, Riyyadus Salihin headed by Amir Khamzat, and Doku

1

Umarov's Caucasus Emirate, established in 2007 and declared a terrorist organization by the U.S. State Department on May 26, 2011.[2] The goals of these groups include: 1) discourage Russian authorities from fighting the terrorists, who have a "long-war" strategy to bog down their adversaries with attacks on military and civilian targets; 2) spread Islamist ideology "by example" and recruit North Caucasus youth for the "holy war" against Russia as well as for global jihad; and, 3) fight to create the "Caucasus emirate" (*Imarat Kavkaz*). The latter is a self-proclaimed state entity that would stretch over the entire North Caucasus. Its main goal is to secede from Russia and form an independent state, ruled by Sharia law.

Terrorism in the North Caucasus was pioneered by the Chechen fighters in the 1990s, when forces commanded by Shamil Basayev executed Pervomaysk and Budyonnovsk attacks. In Budyonnovsk in June 1995, 195 terrorists led by Basayev took around 1,500 civilians hostage in the village in the Stavropol District. As a result of the attack, 129 people were killed and 415 injured. The operation was a success for the terrorists, who released the hostages after Moscow granted them a safe passage to Chechnya. In Pervomaysk in January 1996, a group of rebel fighters took 36 policemen hostage while trying to cross the nearby border into Chechnya. They managed to escape the several-day siege of the village conducted by the Russian military and made it to Chechnya, albeit with significant casualties (153 out of several hundred rebel fighters were killed).[3]

The astonishing Dubrovka Theater siege in 2002, the 2005 Beslan school massacre, and the 2011 Domodedovo Airport bombing represent the extent to which North Caucasian terrorists are ready to fight and kill for global jihad. However, it appears that the Islamist fighters adjust their tactics and occasionally respond to public criticism. For instance, Doku Umarov has publicly stated that he ordered his fighters to stop civilian attacks.[4] He justified the order by stating that Russian civil society does not support the Putin regime and is its hostage in the same way as the Chechen fighters are for their independence. Nevertheless, the threat to Russia and the world, including civilians, remains severe.

In order to provide adequate policy, military, and security solutions, U.S. military planners and security providers should understand the history, geography, politics, and religious conflicts that are pertinent to the issue at hand. This is what this monograph attempts to accomplish.

HISTORY OF WARFARE AND COUNTERINSURGENCY ALONG RUSSIA'S CAUCASUS BORDERLANDS

Russia and the nations of the Northern Caucasus have been in perpetual conflict since the 18th century, when Russia's military under Catherine the Great annexed the region into the Russian Empire. From the first Russian invasions of the area in the early 18th century through the Caucasian War of 1817 to 1864, historians and novelists, such as Leo Tolstoy (the author of *Hadji Murat*, a short novel) have depicted the numerous battles between the Russians and the nations that make up the Caucasus and their complex relationships.[5] Tolstoy writes:

> The red-haired Gamzalo was the only one Loris-Melikov [a Russian official, A.C.] did not understand. He

saw that that man was not only loyal to Shamil but felt an insuperable aversion, contempt, repugnance, and hatred for all Russians, and Loris-Melikov could therefore not understand why he had come over to them. It occurred to him that, as some of the higher officials suspected, Hadji Murad's surrender and his tales of hatred of Shamil [the rebel commander, A.C.] might be false, and that perhaps he had surrendered only to spy out the Russians' weak spots that, after escaping back to the mountains, he might be able to direct his forces accordingly. Gamzalo's whole person strengthened this suspicion.[6]

Imperial Russia and subsequently the Soviet Union have had a substantial impact on the history, identity, and development of the entire Caucasus. Tsarist Russia needed North Caucasus to secure its connections to and the rule over Southern Caucasus, to establish a bridgehead against the Ottoman Empire and Iran, and to extend its Black Sea coastline. To capture Northern Caucasus, Russia used extensive military force, ethnic cleansing, agricultural colonization, and oppression to force the local Islamic tribes under its rule.[7]

However, since the first battles in the 18th century through the present day, Russia has failed to fully and effectively suppress the separatist tendencies of the Northern Caucasian peoples, who have maintained their culture, language, Islamic religion, and therefore, a distinct and at times hostile identity from Slavic Orthodox Russians.

Islam has been an integral part of Northern Caucasian identity since the late-7th century,[8] when Arab conquerors first introduced it to the region. Some local tribes adopted the religion later than others. The first to do so were those in Dagestan, specifically the Avars and Lezgins, and this slow Islamization lasted from roughly the 8th to the 12th centuries. Chechens were much later, adopting Islam during the 15th and 16th centuries, while the nations of the Western part of the North Caucasus finally did so 2 centuries later.[9] Meanwhile, their southern neighbors Georgia and Armenia continued to follow the Christian Orthodox tradition, each having its own autocephalous Church. For an illustration of ethnic divisions in North Caucasus, see Map 1.

Map 1. North Caucasus Ethnic Divisions.[10]

Despite elements of paganism among the tribes, and Islam not being as fundamentalist as in other areas, Islam was and remains a significant factor that helped unify the many diverse ethnic groups of the fragmented region. As seen on Map 1, the Caucasus is home to a variegated collection of tribes, nations, and cultures that have lived in a small area for centuries with continuous intertribal strife and limited interethnic mixing. Each of the empires, Russian, Ottoman, Iranian, and Mongol, that have occupied the region left visible legacies.

Russia's Use of Overwhelming Force.

In order to open military maneuver space in the South Caucasus, Black Sea area, and to prepare bridgeheads for the onslaught against the declining Ottoman Empire, Russian imperial forces began their invasions of the North Caucasus starting in the 18th century and continuing into the 19th century. The imperial Army and the Cossacks primarily used brutal, overwhelming force that resulted in the complete devastation of villages and towns with high numbers of deaths and refugees.[11]

During the Caucasus war, General Alexei Petrovich Yermolov, the most prominent Russian general in the field, used the tactic of carrots and sticks. As a stick to punish Chechen rebels committing crimes against the Russians, he used ethnic cleansing, burned down villages, and cut down forests. He would order attacks even if he knew that Russian losses would be significant. Yermolov punished the rebellious Chechens by burning their villages, destroying their forces, beating them in skirmishes that never developed into battles, and, occasionally even seeking to win them over by an unwanted display of clemency.[12]

He writes in his memoirs:

> In order to punish the Chechens who were constantly robbing villages, . . . I wanted to turn them out of the Aksayev lands, which they inhabited. . . . I knew that attacking their villages in hardly accessible and forest areas would lead to significant casualties on our side, if the villagers did not remove their wives, children and property first; they always protect these desperately, and only an example of an horror can induce them to do so.[13]

Yermolov also used the "scorched earth" approach, burning all occupied territories to ashes in order to prevent the deported population from being tempted to recolonize the places they once inhabited. Hostile tribes were pushed high into the mountains where many starved, while others were forced to settle in Russian-controlled lowlands. These tactics gave Russia the upper hand and facilitated the subjugation of the North Caucasus peoples. With these actions, Yermolov and his disciples planted the seeds of future hatred between the highlanders of the Caucasus and the Russians.

Yermolov also made use of carrots, attempting to lure the local elites to the Russian side through various gifts and concessions. The local elites were recruited to serve the Russians, and were given salaries as if they represented the Russian leadership in the areas they controlled.[14] Cooptation of and cooperation with local ethnic elites was a cornerstone of the Russian empire in general. In other words, Russian leadership used their counterparts from the ethnic groups they came to dominate to ensure metropolitan rule.

Another tactic worth mentioning is the frequent use of *abatises* (Rus. *zaseki*). These were obstacles formed with the branches of trees laid in a row, with the sharpened ends directed toward the enemy. The trees are usually interlaced or tied with wire. I. Drozdov, a contemporary Russian officer, writes that the Russian troops built *abatises* immediately upon arriving at the location of their temporary camp.[15] Once the highlanders attacked these defensive obstacles, they became an easy target for Russian shooters hidden behind them.

Yet, the highlanders fought back. Imam Shamil, a political and religious leader of the Muslim tribes of the North Caucasus, put up the most fierce resistance against the powerful Russian army for 25 years (1834-59). Initially, he tried to avoid direct battles with the Russian forces as he recognized that his position was not sound enough, and he did not wish to waste lives. Instead, he concentrated on solving internal problems, and for a period of time he was able to concentrate his power and avoid major confrontations with the Russian forces. Vladimir Degoyev, a Russian historian and a contemporary scholar of North Caucasus history, quotes Shamil, who described his hit-and-run tactics as "hare's run."[16] Over time, the radical members of the imamate intensified pressure on Shamil to revise these tactics and become more aggressive.

In the early-1840s, Shamil's charismatic leadership allowed him to mobilize an army of more than 10,000 men within days. This newly realized strength, combined with the pressure from the local elite, motivated Shamil to abandon the "hare's run" approach and take advantage of the momentum to initiate broad offensive actions against the Russians. He hurried to consolidate his gains and conquer new territories. He led the war against the Russians as *razziya*, a holy war in the name of Allah (also known as armed jihad or the holy war), and known by its Russian/Caucasus equivalent term, *gazavat*. By proclaiming liberation from the oppression of the infidel, Shamil facilitated the consolidation of his power over his newly conquered lands.

Vladimir Degoyev writes:

> He [Shamil] . . . had a character that could not be impressed by personal material benefits, which so much satisfied other rulers with not so much integrity and which were something that could be traded with Russia. Because of this very reason, it was incomparably easier for Russia to deal with feudal lords than to deal with Shamil. Political, state, ideological and cultural conceptions of Shamil and Russia diverged completely, leaving no space for an effective compromise. Russia was an obstacle for Shamil, just like Shamil was an obstacle for Russia.[17]

Unlike the Russian wars with Turkey and Iran, wars with Shamil were more difficult, due to his unexpected tactics deemed "barbarian" by the Russians. Degoyev writes that the more the Russian generals adhered to the conventional tactics they were taught, the more losses they suffered. Shamil forced the Russians to fight an unconventional war, to which they had trouble adapting. His military talent was based on taking advantage of the unique flexibility of his troops and on understanding the impossibility of defeating the Russians in an open battle. Despite the impression that Shamil's tactics lacked coherence, he always had a plan that took into account the peculiarities of each battle, especially the terrain. He usually attacked the flanks and the rear first, avoiding head-on clashes. Shamil also paid due attention to defense. He built a series of defensive posts, each of which was meant to weaken and exhaust the enemy.

Examples of such tactical successes include the Ichkerinsky Battle in 1842 and the Battle of Dargo in May and June 1845. The Ichkerinsky Battle took place from May 30 to June 2, and the Chechens used tactics of "loose formation" (Rus. *rassypnoy stroy*) and "migrating artillery," consisting mostly of captured cannons.[18] The Russians tried to take advantage of the fact that the main forces of Imam Shamil were in Dagestan at that time. Nevertheless, the Russians under the command of Adjutant-General Pavel Grabbe had to withdraw after losing 66 officers.

In the Battle of Dargo, Shamil and the highlanders again avoided direct clashes with the Russians. They constructed a series of fortifications, which gave them time to fire at the enemy as they were overcoming each obstacle. These tactics increased the number of Russian casualties but were insufficient to keep the Russians out of Dargo. On July 6, 1845, Dargo was conquered by the Russians.[19] Before abandoning the city, they burned it to the ground.

During the 17th to the 19th centuries, the flatlands north of the Terek River gradually came under control of the Cossack settlements and the Russian military.[20] While the Russians were able to inflict serious damage, the mountainous terrain south of the Terek proved very difficult for the imperial military. Chechen and forces of other nations resisting the Russians could hide and organize in the mountains while defending themselves from the advancing forces. This enabled the North Caucasus to battle the Russian invasion forces long after the annexation of Georgia in 1801, Armenia in the early-1810s, and Azerbaijan in the late-1820s.[21]

Beyond military subjugation, the Russian Empire did not have a cohesive strategy to introduce the Russian culture through "soft-power" means that would seek to attract peoples of the Caucasus to their orbit. Instead, in parts of the region, the main goal of the Russian leadership was to "liberate" the Caucasus from the local indigenous people via ethnic cleansing.[22] New Russian settlements were built on the territories emptied by the advancing forces. These settlements were to serve as a means of an eventual full Russification of the region and for further penetrating into the mountainous territories.

In order to secure the area around the settlements, large amounts of forests were cut down, forcing the locals to abandon their comfortable living areas in the lowlands. As I. Drozdov, a Russian officer and eye witness, wrote in 1877:

> In late February [1864] the Pshekh battalion moved to the river of Marte in order to observe how the mountain dwellers were being deported, and, if necessary, in order to evict them by force. . . . The view was atrocious: scattered corpses of children, women and elders, torn, eaten by dogs; migrants exhausted by famine and diseases, who could barely move, kept falling on the ground out of exhaustion, being eaten alive by hungry dogs. . . . On May 28, 1864, the Caucasian war was over. The Kuban Oblast' [roughly corresponding to today's Krasnodar Kray–A.C.] was conquered as well as "cleansed." Only a handful of people were left out of a formerly large population that once lived there.[23]

Russia had limited means to introduce the Christian Orthodox religion as a meaningful alternative to Islam, since the Caucasian ethnic groups, and especially their leaders, used Islam as a unifying force against the Russians. Thus, the highlander tribes would never accept the Russian Orthodox Church, as it was the faith of the "infidel enemy."[24]

With a limited "soft-power" tool box, tsarist Russia had to rely on violence and the destruction of the North Caucasus tribes to control the region. Though they managed to colonize the region outright, military power never fully extinguished the desire among indigenous peoples to shake off the Russian yoke. One of the North Caucasus nations that was a victim of the Russian expansionary policy was the Circassians. The tragedy of the Circassians was that they were unable to unite against the common enemy. The 12 stars on the current flag of Adygea symbolize the 12 original Circassian tribes, although their real number was allegedly even higher.[25] A prince led each tribe, and the number of internal disputes among the tribes was significant. Their divisiveness determined the outcome of their war against the Russian forces. Having lost, entire Circassian clans were forced to flee their homeland, and most of them did not survive. They either drowned in the sea on their way to Anatolia when the overloaded Turkish boats sank, or died from hunger and diseases in relocation camps.[26]

It is worth noting that Russia was not the only power that used harsh methods to enlarge its territory and subjugate the people that lived along its perimeter or in the colonies. The 19th century was one of struggle of large powers for dominance, and similar approaches were used by other empires, such as the British, French, Ottoman, as well as the expanding United States.

AFTER WORLD WAR I

Following World War I and during the Russian Civil War (1918-21), Chechnya initially supported tsarist forces. However, later it switched sides and supported the Bolsheviks. The reason for this was a series of myopic mistakes made by General Anton Denikin, the commander of the anti-communist (White) southern Russian forces, in his treatment of the North Caucasus nations. First, Denikin ignored the level of alienation and the atheism the Bolsheviks imposed on the traditional life of the Muslim highlanders. Second, blinded by the imperialism permeating other tsarist generals ("Russia one and undivided"), Denikin and his men turned the highlander peoples against them.[27] The White forces myopically viewed this strategy as a new conquest of the Caucasus, which did not allow for alliances with the local Chechen and Ingush leadership, who initially were willing to fight the Red Army on the side of the Whites.

Practical actions of Denikin only intensified the alienation of the North Caucasus people from the White army. He punished the Chechens and wanted them to "pay back" for all losses suffered by the Don and Kuban Cossacks, who fought on the tsarist side. Both the Chechens and the Ingush responded with a fierce resistance and expelled Denikin's forces from the area. Other strategic mistakes added to the Chechen and Ingush defiance. Just like Yermolov more than half a century before him, Denikin made use of "scorched earth" tactics, which further alienated the North Caucasian nationalities.[28]

The new Soviet leadership made its own mistakes in the North Caucasus. It was openly hostile toward Islam, rudely ignored the mountaineers' traditions and used the total expropriation approach of "military communism" that existed in Russia in 1918–21.[29] They provided for the abolition of private banks, nationalization of industry, central planning, government monopoly on commerce, equal distribution of material goods, and mandatory labor.[30] This approach of the Communists quickly cooled down the enthusiasm of the mountaineers, who initially welcomed the arrival of the Red Army. However, despite their mistakes, the Soviets were willing, at least on paper, to grant them a certain level of autonomy, proclaimed in the Declaration of the Rights of the Peoples of Russia.[31] Despite their promises, disillusionment with the Red dictatorship set in quickly.

Stalin Cracks Down.

During the time of the Russian Civil War (1918-21) and the establishment of the Soviet Union (1922), the Red Army crushed the Caucasian revolt with mercilessness similar to that of the Tsar. After the defeat of the White Armies, including the ones of the Don and the Kuban Cossacks, the Soviet Union retained ethnic Russians' dominance over the region using the new military technologies of World War I: tanks, airpower, modern artillery, and chemical weapons. The Caucasus tribes, on the other hand, were primarily using the same weapons they had in the 18th and 19th centuries.[32]

Then an ethnic Georgian, Joseph Stalin, born Iosif (Soso) Djugashvili in the Georgian town of Gori, became, first, the Commissar for Nationalities, and then the leader of the Soviet Union. The peoples of the Caucasus entered into a new chapter of relations with Moscow that would soon see their nations torn out at the roots.

As World War II raged, Stalin accused North-ern Caucasus peoples, especially Chechens, Ingush, Karachays, and Balkars (as well as Kalmyks and Crimean Tatars), of treason against the state and alleged collusion with the Nazis, despite the lack of any credible evidence.[33] Although many Caucasian highlanders fought valiantly in the Red Army in World War II, Stalin punished even veterans, their families, and their nations with death, imprisonment, and brutal relocation to Siberia and Central Asia. In this ethnic cleansing, up to one-third of Chechens died.

The operation aimed at deporting the Chechens and the Ingush from their homes in the North Caucasus, called Operation LENTIL, started in February 1944. According to a cable sent to Stalin by Beria, who personally supervised the expulsion, 478,479 Chechens and Ingush were deported within the first week of the operation.[34] The data on the total number of deported people vary. A cable sent to Stalin in July 1944 states that 602,193 people were moved from the North Caucasus into the Kazakh and Kyrgyz Soviet Socialist Republics, most of whom were Chechens and Ingush (428,948), followed by Karachays (68,327) and Balkars (37,406). Another cable lists the total number of deported Chechens, Ingush, Kalmyks, and Karachays as 650,000.[35]

The excuse and formal justification to undertake these deportations varied from nation to nation, but were of a similar nature. For instance, the Karachays were accused of "treacherous behavior, joining German-organized battalions in order to fight the Soviet leadership, betraying honest Soviet citizens to the Germans, accompanying the German troops and showing them the way. . ."[36] After the end of the war, they were accused of "resisting Soviet actions," and "hiding bandits and German agents." Kalmyks were charged with "betraying the Motherland, joining German battalions in order to fight the Red Army, betraying honest Soviet citizens to the Germans, and giving the Germans communal cattle from the Rostov Oblast and Ukraine." Similarly to the Karachays after the war the Kalmyks were accused of "actively resisting Soviet efforts of rebuilding the economy destroyed by the Germans" and "terrorizing the surrounding population."[37] Crimean Tatars were allegedly guilty of "treacherous actions against the Soviet nation."[38]

Like his tsarist predecessors, in the place of the "punished" groups, Stalin resettled ethnic Russians in order to dominate the indigenous ethnicities through demographic warfare rather than conventional warfare alone. Since the Soviet Union mandated an atheist society, the Kremlin also cracked down on Islam, cutting ties with overseas institutions of learning and banning Hajj. Stalin's idea was to change North Caucasian tribal and Islamic civilization and culture to the socialist realist fare the rest of the country was already experiencing. The communist party shut down mosques, hounded mullahs, destroyed Buddhist monasteries of the Kalmyks, and murdered or imprisoned the lamas.

After Nikita Khrushchev's recognition of Stalin's atrocities and the "cult of personality," he allowed exiled Chechen, Ingush, and others to return to their native lands from the exile as a part of Khrushchev's "thaw" policies during his reign. While many (but not all) returned to their ancestral homelands, they still were unable to fully practice their religion and some of their cultural traditions due to the restrictions placed on all Soviet citizens. As a result, the remnants of their customs went underground; however, as tribal elders found great difficulty in transferring their traditions and practices to the young, after repatriation in 1956-57, North Caucasus became bereft of cultural and religious leaders who would preserve the Islamic Sufi tradition during post-Stalinist Soviet period.[39] This religious and cultural vacuum in the region became fertile grounds for the new Salafi forms of Islam that infiltrated North Caucasus in 1990s, and encountered little competition from the traditional, moderate forms of Islam.[40]

COLLAPSE OF THE UNION OF SOVIET SOCIALIST REPUBLICS AND THE FIRST CHECHEN WAR (LATE-1980s TO 1994)

During the last years of the Soviet Union through the early years of the Russian Federation, Chechnya and Dagestan showed the most prolific renaissance of Islam and nationalism among all the Northern Caucasus. With the Soviet ideological control beginning to disappear, most people in the region revived their sense of religious, ethnic, and cultural identity, which had existed before the USSR. One reason for the quick rise in nationalism and the quest for independence was the impact of the tsarist oppression and Stalinist expulsions. Though not the only ethnic group to suffer from ethnic cleansing by the Romanoff empire or Soviet Russia, the Chechen leadership of the early-1990s consisted of figures who were born and/or raised in exile in Kazakhstan — and bore the grudge.[41]

Nationalism and the bitter memories that united the Chechen people against the Moscow-based Russian government created the strong yearning for Chechen independence, while other Caucasian republics were less rebellious. In addition, from the 1980s through the 1990s, Islam was going through a renaissance. All of the North Caucasus republics experienced an increase in Islamic activity, partly as a result of *"glasnost"* and the Russians' inability to regulate religion and partly due to opening of the borders to outgoing and incoming religiously-related travel, including Hajj and study abroad.[42]

New forms of Islam, however, had origins outside of the region. The newly introduced Salafi/Wahhabi sects were radical and had roots in Saudi Arabia and in Salafism throughout the Middle East and Pakistan. These imported religious teachers were well-financed, and their following drew on the fanaticism and enthusiasm of the separatists, ready to use force and faith to achieve their goals. Initially, most of North Caucasus society, especially the elders, rejected these Islamist imports. They had no desire to adopt novel forms of Islam built on radicalism that would seek to overhaul the traditions that the region had fought to uphold for generations and sought to preserve and to resurrect. Meanwhile, many younger people had little knowledge and appreciation of the historical connections between themselves and their heritage, which made them vulnerable to radical Islam's influence and appeal.[43]

In the early-1990s, the socio-economic situation in the Soviet Union/Russia and the Northern Caucasus sharply deteriorated, undermining the hopes for a peaceful and prosperous post-Soviet future while quietly integrating into post-communist Russian Federation. The chaotic disintegration of the Soviet Union led to the independence of 14 republics and to the creation of the Russian Federation under the leadership of Boris Yeltsin.

In the South Caucasus, the former Soviet Socialist Republics of the USSR, Armenia, Georgia, and Azerbaijan became independent states in 1991. The North Caucasus region consisted of Autonomous Soviet Socialist Republics (ASSRs), which were subordinate to the Russian Soviet Federative Socialist Republic (RSFSR). When the Soviet Union dissolved, Moscow would not authorize these nations, which constituted autonomous republics, to create sovereign states.[44]

As a result of the breakup of the Soviet Union, Moscow witnessed the loss of its empire, including regions that had both a geostrategic value and were considered legitimately under Russian control due to decades spent conquering them. President Yeltsin and the majority of Russian elites, including liberals and nationalists, believed that further losses of Russian territory to secession of various national-territorial autonomous republics could bring about the disintegration of the Russian historic core. Needing to preserve what was left of the "Motherland," Yeltsin could not afford to yield independence to any rebel territory. His famous phrase, "take as much sovereignty as you can carry away," applied to pacific lands, willing to patiently and peacefully negotiate disagreements, such as Tatarstan, not the rebel Chechnya.[45]

Thus, Russia's approach to post-Soviet Chechnya has been a mix of modern strategic goals of state preservation and resistance to centrifugal processes, together with obsolescent military tactics of overwhelming, imprecise fire power, ham-handed counterinsurgency, and roots dating back to the Caucasus wars of the 18th and 19th centuries.

Around the time of the dissolution of the Soviet Union, former Soviet Air Force general Dzhokhar Dudayev, an ethnic Chechen, was elected president of the Autonomous Republic of Chechnya on October 27, 1991, which remained a part of the new Russian Federation. He gained 90.1 percent of the votes,[46] although his opponents accused him of falsifying the results. Upon witnessing the independence of former Soviet satellites in Eastern Europe and Union republics, some of them smaller than Chechnya, Dudayev declared Chechnya independent as the Chechen Republic of Ichkeria immediately upon his election.[47]

With the Chechen declaration of independence and the Russian resistance, both sides reverted to an active state of hostility. On November 8, Yeltsin issued a decree declaring a state of emergency in Chechnya. In 1992, Russia and the Chechen separatists held several rounds of fruitless talks dedicated to the normalization of relations. The year 1993 can be characterized by the Kremlin's confrontation with the rebellious anti-Yeltsin parliament, making integration impossible. After a period of a *de facto* Chechen independence in 1991–94, in the fall of 1994 Yeltsin and his administration refocused on the North Caucasus. In December 1994, Moscow re-invaded Chechnya.

The First Chechen War (1994-96).

The conditions at the beginning of the First Chechen War were similar to many cases of decolonization worldwide. The metropolis was weakened by internal strife, while the peripheral elite desired to shake loose the imperial chains. Relations between Chechnya and Russia were contentious. Svante E. Cornell points out that the Chechen military elite was not interested in a negotiated dialogue with Moscow to create a compromise that would allow Chechnya to live in peaceful coexistence within the Russian Federation.[48] In fact, other Muslim-majority regions like Tatarstan, Bashkortostan, and many of the North Caucasian republics managed to come to agreements with President Yeltsin on their constitutional status.[49] Several reasons can explain this difference. First, compared to the other Russian republics, Chechnya's population is highly homogenous. According to the 2002 census, the share of Chechens was 93.5 percent.[50] In contrast, only 52.9 percent of the population of Tatarstan was Tatars and almost 40 percent were Russians. Similarly, in Bashkortostan, the largest ethnic group in 2002 was the Russians (36.1 percent), followed by the Bashkirs (29.5 percent) and Tatars (25.4 percent). Russians in Dagestan constituted only 4.7 percent of the population in 2002. However, the population of Dagestan does not have a majority ethnic group, but instead is made up of several main nationalities, such as the Avars (29.4 percent), Dargyns (16.5 percent), and Kumiks (14.2 percent). It was more difficult for the non-Russian populations of Tatarstan, Bashkortostan, and most other republics of the RSFSR to organize strong movements for independence, since they did not have a dominant ethnic group as a secessionist support base.

Second, Chechen separatists were supported by outside forces. According to a Russian source, foreign mercenaries from 15 countries fought the Russian federal forces in the First Chechen War.[51] In the Second Chechen War of 1999–2000, the number of the countries represented rose to 52. In 2000, the number of foreign mercenaries reached 600–700 people.

Third, the Chechen leadership was set against any deal with Russia. In his last interview, former Russian defense minister Pavel Grachev discusses how neither he nor Dudayev wanted war.[52] Grachev says Dudayev must have reacted (by declaring independence), because Moscow flatly refused to talk to him, and in such a situation, the Chechen leadership and nation would reject Dudayev's inaction.

The majority of the Chechen elite believed that independence was the sole option, and that their people could live freely and peacefully only if they had a clean break from Russia.[53] This enduring political philosophy among the Chechens was very similar to their unwillingness to compromise with imperial Russian forces, beginning with the first invasions in the 18th century and to their refusal to acquiesce to Russia's occupation ever since. The Stalinist expulsions in the 1940s and the attempted eradication of Islam in the region only confirmed what the Chechens believed for centuries: The Russians could not be relied upon to protect them and to ensure their freedom to live how they wish.

Nonetheless, the negotiations lasted from March 1992 to January 1993, but the talks ultimately failed.[54] The Kremlin then tried to implement a "coercive diplomacy" approach by adopting a more belligerent tone toward the Chechen leaders in an attempt to compel them to make a deal similar to their other Muslim counterparts, but these efforts also failed. In November 1994, the Russians tried to execute a coup against Dudayev, in part by organizing pro-Moscow Chechens to oust their leader.[55] The attempted coup was a massive defeat for the Russians.

Before the war, Defense Minister Grachev made a failed attempt to transform the North Caucasus into a buffer military district meant to shield Russia from the instability in the South Caucasus. This step would mean sending the best battalions into the region. What happened in reality was the exact opposite. Most of the battalions moved to the North Caucasus were unprepared for the war and almost totally lost their fighting ability during the war. Trying to contain this negative trend, the military leadership tried to put together battalions that were still able to fight, but even this strategy turned out to be insufficient to defeat the Chechen guerilla fighters.

Following the series of failures, Moscow intensified its efforts. The Russian military leadership misinterpreted the Dudayev government's lack of engagement with pro-Moscow Chechens as a weakness or a haplessness on the part of the separatists. They did not realize, according to Ilyas Akhmadov and Miriam Lanskoy *et al.*, that the Chechens were hesitant to kill each other in the fear that this would spark blood feuds and vendettas between Chechen clans that had plagued the nation centuries before.[56] Vendettas are a part of the tribal culture of the Caucasus Mountains.

In part, as a result of this miscalculation, Russian forces assumed that any incursion into Grozny would be easy and incur with minimal Russian casualties. They were wrong. For the ill-fated November 1994 invasion, the Federal Counterintelligence Service had assembled elite tank squadrons for an attack on Grozny. Chechen forces ambushed them with ease and took many Russian soldiers as prisoners. This failure sparked criticism of then-defense minister Pavel Grachev, who had famously said that he would capture Grozny with one paratroops battalion in 2 hours.[57] He later justified his statement by stating that it would really have been possible providing that he could fight by all the rules of warfare, meaning the availability of unlimited aviation, artillery, etc. In such case, he claimed, the remaining rebel fighter bands could have really been destroyed or captured with one airborne battalion. But this was an ex-post-facto justification.

The Russian reaction to the humiliating failure to capture Grozny was to boost its forces and essentially declare war, retake Chechnya, and restore Russian pride and control. The Russian assault on Grozny began in December 1994 and was met with heavy resistance from the Chechen forces on the ground. In order to engulf Chechnya in a "shock-and-awe" assault, the Russian military subjected Grozny and other major Chechen cities to an intense air bombardment that all but obliterated them, resulting in tens of thousands of civilian casualties and hundreds of thousands of refugees.[58] They were the first Russian cities destroyed since World War II—and as utterly as the cities obliterated by the Nazis.

After 2 months of initial engagement, the Russian army conquered most of Chechnya and forced the separatists to flee into the southern mountains, where they regrouped.[59] Despite Dudayev's assassination in April 1996 by a Russian precision-guided missile, Chechen forces successfully recaptured Grozny from the Russians after a few days of fighting; both sides signed a cease-fire agreement known as the Khasavyurt Accord a few weeks thereafter.[60]

During this war, the Chechen rebels launched their first terrorist attack and hostage standoff on a hospital in Budyonnovsk in Stavopolsky Krai. The guerilla commando unit, led by Shamil Basayev, consisted of about 150 Chechen rebels. On June 14, 1995, the terrorists stormed the unguarded hospital and took 2,000 hostages.[61] The Russian Special Forces were called in the following day,[62] and the operation to neutralize the rebels was launched on June 17. However, it failed to completely liberate the hospital. On June 18, Prime Minister Viktor Chernomyrdin negotiated with Basayev over the phone and accepted some of Basayev's demands, including a safe passage to Chechnya. During the siege, 129 people died and 415 were injured.[63] This is the earliest terrorist attack credited to the Chechens, and is believed to have reinvigorated the fight against the Russians.[64] This is also the largest hostage taking event ever to occur in Russian territory.[65]

The Chechen Tactics.

An important figure that supported the Chechens in their separatist efforts against Moscow was Ibn al-Khattab, a Saudi citizen who joined the Chechen war in late 1994. Khattab secured international financing of the separatists, procuring weapons and building terrorist preparation camps in Chechnya. One of the most important elements of the hostilities in Chechnya was a sniper war. Snipers were heavily relied upon on the Chechen side, and the Russian federal forces responded in the same way.

The Chechen separatists avoided direct contact with the Russian forces. They preferred operating in small units of three to five people.[66] These units included a sniper, an rocket-propelled grenade (RPG) operator/grenade launcher, a machine gunner, and one or two submachine gunners. Their tactics were as follows: the main group opens fire at the federal forces, while a sniper, often hidden in a tree and shielded by the noise of the battle, neutralizes them. The separatists preferred short and frequent fire engagements to avoid casualties.

The tactics of "fighting troikas" (Rus. *boyevaya troika*) deserve special attention. It consisted of one sniper, one grenade launcher, and one submachine gunner. In a military operation, the gunner initiated the battle by opening fire at the enemy to provoke them to fire back. The sniper identified the sources of the enemy's fire and destroyed them. Meanwhile, the grenade launcher destroyed armored vehicles and machinery. If the fighting troika was on the defense, it quickly ambushed the Russian forces and hid in the surrounding area. Once the Russian attack began, the separatists were able to shoot at the enemy soldiers from their hiding places only a short distance (100–150 yards) away. Snipers targeted the Russian commanders and the most active soldiers in order to spread panic among the Russian troops.

The Chechens also widely used wounded Russian troops as "bait." They intentionally did not kill them, but waited to ambush the Russian soldiers who came to help their wounded comrades. Once the number of the wounded Russian troops was large enough, the Chechens systematically killed them.

The Russians used a combination of carrots and sticks.[67] The Russian leadership led an active campaign among the Chechen population, calling upon it to persuade the rebels to leave their villages. Meanwhile, the Russians kept taking control of high grounds around Chechen towns, which rendered any armed resistance meaningless. These tactics allowed the Russians to capture the towns of Argun, Gudermes, and Shali without fighting in 1995.

In battles, the Russians used massive fire barrages, which turned out to be a wrong strategy for the type of warfare they faced in Chechnya.[68] Russian generals were using strategies that would be appropriate in a large-scale military operation with a clearly defined battlefront, but not for guerilla war in Chechnya. Chechen battalions were highly mobile; they kept splitting into smaller subunits, which later reunited.

This Russian miscalculation, together with a superior knowledge of the mountain landscape, allowed the Chechens to avoid Russian artillery fire and air strikes. There was no clear battlefront, and the federal forces had to bomb civilian objects, causing noncombatant casualties and uniting the Chechen people against the Russian military. In other words, the Russians were repeating the mistakes of their 19th-century forefathers, American commanders in Vietnam, and the Soviets in Afghanistan.

With the training that Chechen leaders received while in the Soviet military, including fighting in Afghanistan, the experiences some guerilla elements such as Shamil Basayev had in fighting on the Russian side against Georgians in Abkhazia and Armenians in Nagorno-Karabakh—together with the abundance of Soviet-era weaponry and better motivated troops— gave Chechnya an advantage. Training provided by al-Qaeda and other affiliated militant Islamists also played an important role. For example, Shamil Basayev came to Afghanistan in 1994 and visited training camps in the province of Khost.[69] He later received training by and was in regular contact with al-Qaeda. In total, several hundreds of Chechens were trained in al-Qaeda camps in Afghanistan, and militant Islamist groups also financially supported the recruitment of fighters from neighboring Georgia and Azerbaijan.

Air power proved not to be the decisive factor expected to win the First Chechen War. The overreliance on air power and its failure led to the Russian troops being poorly supplied and trained, inadequately led, demoralized, exhausted, and disorganized. In *One Soldier's War*, his memoir of Russian army life, Arkady Babchenko writes:

We stopped caring for ourselves, no longer washed, shaved or brushed our teeth. After a week without soap and water, our hands cracked and bled continually, blighted by eczema in the cold. We hadn't warmed ourselves by a fire for a whole week because the damp reeds wouldn't burn and there was nowhere to gather firewood in the steppe. We began to turn wild as the cold and wet and filth drove from us all feelings apart from hatred, and we hated everything on earth, including ourselves.[70]

The Chechens used creative tactics to defeat the Russians in the city centers. As described in a RAND Corporation report by Arthur L. Speyer III, the Chechen strategy in the cities was a "textbook example of the modern urban guerilla."[71] In order to minimize casualties, the Russians would use tanks and air forces without infantry to bombard various buildings where rebels were believed to be hiding.[72] Once Russian forces were deeply enmeshed in the city, the Chechens would attack from positions in buildings alongside the city streets, greatly relying on tried-and-tested Russian RPGs used in packs.[73] The entrances to these buildings were barricaded from the inside, and the top floors were unoccupied so that air attacks would yield the least amount of Chechen casualties.[74]

The Russian command failed to fully take into account that even if the Chechens are forced to relinquish temporary control of their cities and plains, they were likely to recover while waiting out the enemy in the mountains and come back with a vengeance, utilizing their mountainous guerilla-style tactics.

The Chechens had a significant intelligence advantage because their leaders, including the Grozny city engineer, had been preparing for an invasion of the city for 2 years. Russian intelligence performed woefully, due to the lack of local sources and their inability to fight an enemy whose language and traditions the ethnic Slavs were not familiar with and whom they underestimated due to the darker hue of their skin. Using tanks and planes in lieu of infantry to storm each building led to the bogging down of the Russian operations and their ultimate withdrawal in 1996.

The First Chechen War was a spectacularly demoralizing defeat for the Russian political leadership and the Russian military, which itself was undergoing an identity crisis after the collapse of the Soviet Union. The strategy included an overwhelming use of air power to destroy cities, kill and terrorize civilians, and demolish the power centers of the Chechen separatists. This approach was counterproductive because it caused severe civilian casualties and radicalized many of those who remained neutral or even supported remaining a part of Russia.

The Russian General Staff did not realize that the Chechens were trained by Islamist emissaries; the training would be expanded in the interwar period of 1996-99 during the presidency of Aslan Maskhadov.

ASLAN MASKHADOV AND THE INTERWAR PERIOD

In 1997, Colonel Aslan Maskhadov, an ex-Soviet artillery officer who fought valiantly in the First Chechen War, was elected president of the separatist Chechen Republic of Ichkeria. This proved that the ordinary Chechens were tired of the war and hoped Maskhadov would be able to find a compromise with Moscow.[75] Maskhadov, a talented and successful military commander, however, turned out to be a poor politician. He was a hostage of the interests of influential field commanders, such as Shamil Basayev and Salman Raduyev, whose resolve was stronger than Maskhadov's. The centralized economy and social welfare system broke down for good. It was the right of the stronger and the closeness to the sources of financing from Moscow's federal budget that had the ultimate deciding power.

As the president of Ichkeria, Maskhadov continued to think in military terms. He had to choose whether to ally himself with Akhmad Kadyrov, who brought together the opponents of Wahhabism, or Shamil Basayev, who was preparing a military campaign to conquer Dagestan and create a larger state (emirate) under the influence of the Wahhabist ideology. In that, the problems of 1990s are reminiscent of those facing Imam Shamil in 1840s. Maskhadov chose Basayev, backed by the strongest battalions of the Ichkerian military.

During the interwar period, relations between the Chechen separatists and the Taliban continued to thrive.[76] In 1997 and 1998, Zelimkhan Yandarbiyev and Movladi Udugov, two main Chechen terrorist ideologues, visited the Taliban-controlled Afghanistan and held meetings with Mullah Muhammad Omar and Osama bin Laden. Konstantin Kosachev, a former head of the State Duma Committee on International Relations, said, "We have reasons to believe that Osama bin Laden was involved in a series of terrorist attacks in our country."[77]

Russia in the Aftermath of the First Chechen War.

The Russian society was unprepared for what started as a poorly organized military improvization and morphed into the First Chechen War.[78] Due to the lack of understanding of the reasons for the operation, the attitude of the Russian public toward the political leadership that initiated it and the generals that led it was largely negative, and the leadership's credibility was hitting rock bottom. At a later stage of the war, the public pressured Yeltsin to start negotiating with the rebels.[79]

However, the attitude of ordinary Russians toward the ongoing Chechen conflict kept changing, depending on the latest developments in the war. For instance, in late-1995, after the federal forces failed to achieve a breakthrough, as little as 3.2 percent of the people supported continuing the war, while 51.1 percent supported an immediate withdrawal of the troops.[80] In November 1999, 62.5 percent supported continuing the war after the federal forces neutralized Basayev's band and achieved noticeable successes in the republic.[81]

The number of Russian casualties in the First Chechen War was below the threshold that would lead to mass antiwar protests. However, conscription and the deployment of police units from all across the country to fight in Chechnya contributed to a transformation of an initially local conflict into a nationwide one. The return of large numbers of angry and demoralized veterans led to talks about Russia's "Weimar syndrome" in reference to pre-Nazi Germany, where World War I veterans played a significant role in political radicalization.

The military considered itself betrayed by the chaotic actions of the Russian leadership and ostracized by the people. The failure to achieve victory was unexpected by the public, which had gotten used to regarding the Russian military as a formidable force even against Europe and the United States.[82]

Before the start of the war, the supreme military leadership considered the upcoming deployment of troops in Chechnya to be another "peace-keeping" operation, similar in nature to those in, for example, Transnistria.[83]

The peace agreement with Chechnya, signed in 1996, became a symbol of defeat and humiliation of Russia—only 4 years after the inglorious abandonment of Afghanistan. Nevertheless, little energy had been spent to learn from the failed Chechen war. One of the possible reasons is that the military leadership was hesitant to admit its defeat and instead chose to play up the story about the betrayal by the politicians.

After the failed First Chechen War, the Kremlin learned several military lessons. It understood the necessity to estimate the military capabilities of the separatists more objectively and to ensure better collection of and better quality information. The Russian leadership recognized the need for political support for the Army and law enforcement agencies, and that the separatists could not be expected to keep their ends of negotiated bargains due to their decentralized structure.

Overall, the First Chechen War was lost to the well-organized and led Chechen guerillas by an army that did not draw the appropriate conclusions from its defeat in Afghanistan. Russia's failure resonated around the world, and the global reaction to it was surprise and disdain. The communist colossus, which only 10 years earlier had the United States and the world trembling, was defeated by a ragtag army of guerillas in the territory the Russian empire had controlled for over 200 years. The defeat greatly imperiled Russia's ambition to become a leading power in the post-Soviet space and a serious player in the post-Cold-War world order. Nonetheless, Yeltsin, the Kremlin, the military, and the nationalist elite across the board—communists, nationalists, and many liberals—remained committed to defeating the Chechen separatists. They did not have to wait long to get a second chance. After a brief and traumatic interwar period, extremists provoked another disastrous war.

The Interwar Period in the North Caucasus (1996-99).

In the Soviet Union, with its internationalist and atheist ideology collapsed, religion and nationalism began filling the political and spiritual void. While Russians increasingly self-identified as Christian Orthodox Eastern Slavs, their opponents self-identified as Chechens and Sunni Muslims. Dzokhar Dudayev and his de facto Chechen government mainly used separatism and independence as the motivating factors in fighting the Russians. Additionally, traditional Sufi Islam was a stimulus that generated separatist attitudes against the Russians. Traditional Sufi Islam was never isolated from the idea of the Chechen nation, nor was it the primary factor that inspired the Chechen forces to fight against the Russians and to die for Chechnya in 1994-96.

After the end of the First Chechen War, however, nonindigenous forms of Islam such as Salafi/Wahhabi, which were far more radical and global in scope, began to enter aggressively into Chechnya and neighboring North Caucasian republics to exploit the desperate socioeconomic situation in war-torn region. A significant problem that intensified in the period between the two wars was the Islamization of Chechnya. Although Moscow signed a treaty with Chechnya that called for mutual relations based on the principles of international law, Moscow failed to provide sufficient funds to rebuild the Chechen infrastructure damaged or destroyed during the First Chechen War. Social problems resulting from the neglect by Moscow provided a fertile ground for radical Islamic currents, such as Salafism or Wahhabism, to take hold in the republic.[84]

The political course of the acting president Zelimkhan Yandarbiyev in 1996-97, aimed at the rapid Islamization of Chechnya, facilitated the spread of Wahhabism in the republic.[85] In order to strengthen the Sharia law in Chechnya, Bagauddin Magomedov, a radical Islamist leader active in Dagestan, was invited to visit. In September 1996, Yandarbiyev issued a decree that abolished Russian law, banned civil courts, and introduced an Islamic (Sharia) criminal code, which was essentially copied from that of Saudi Arabia.[86] Islam was declared an official religion.

Not all leaders in Chechnya welcomed this new course. The Chechen Islamization was opposed primarily by Aslan Maskhadov and Akhmad Kadyrov. Maskhadov, who was a Prime Minister under Yandarbiyev, did not favor the hasty introduction of Islam as an official religion as he feared that it could lead to a fight for the title of imam, and that the Afghan or Tajik scenarios of a religious war could be repeated in Chechnya. Nevertheless, in his presidential campaign in 1997, Maskhadov, for reasons not entirely clear, used the slogan of creating a "Chechen Islamic state." He might have wanted to steal a popular topic from his political opponents, or perhaps he believed that Sharia law was the only way to unify the fractious Chechens under an overarching ideology. On July 25, 1998, Maskhadov organized a congress of the

Muslims of the North Caucasus in Grozny. Its participants accused the Salafists/Wahhabists of extremism, intervention in the Chechen political life, and insubordination to the official Chechen authorities. He also called upon the Chechen president to get rid of members of his administration who supported this extremist ideology. The chief mufti of Chechnya, Akhmad Kadyrov, also opposed the spreading of Salafism/ Wahhabism in Chechnya. He launched a campaign aimed at discrediting Wahhabism as an alien ideology and its preachers as agents of foreign secret services. Nevertheless, Wahhabism in Chechnya was not eradicated. The Wahhabists allied themselves with other religious radicals, who were proponents of an anti-Russian jihad in the North Caucasus.

The fertile ground for radical Islam also caught the attention of al-Qaeda, which was interested in taking advantage of the situation to expand into new territories. In December 1996, Ayman al-Zawahiri, al-Qaeda's second in command, tried to establish a new base for the organization in Chechnya.[87] He was arrested in Dagestan and released in 1997.

However, the spread of radical Islam was not confined exclusively to Chechnya. In August 1999, rebels under the command of al-Khattab and Basayev invaded two Dagestani regions bordering Chechnya and declared the creation of an Islamic state. In a subsequent Russian military operation, three Wahhabist villages where the radicals had taken hold were destroyed. In the meantime, the territory of Chechnya was targeted by a rocket attack from the federal forces. This invasion of Dagestan led to a full-fledged military operation, known as the Second Chechen War.

Failures on Both Sides.

Russia missed the opportunity to establish a working relationship with moderate nationalists in Chechnya and Dagestan and, facilitated by its high-handed tactics, the Salafist penetration of Chechnya and North Caucasus.

With the economic depression in the region, high unemployment—especially high youth unemployment—and destabilizing forces (ranging from criminal gangs to Islamist terrorists) began to establish safe havens and thrive in interwar Chechnya.[88] The First Chechen War left Chechnya in a disastrous economic situation, in which people had only slim prospects for a bright future. Most of what had remained of the economy was predominantly controlled by the secessionist leaders and their gangs. In this period, the main sources of income for Chechnya were oil, drugs, hostages, and federal subsidies from Moscow.

In the late-1990s, the main source of income for Chechnya (other than federal subsidies) was oil.[89] In 1997, Chechnya produced two million tons of oil annually, according to official statistics. In late 1998, official oil sales in Chechnya were almost totally terminated due to staggering volumes of oil illegally smuggled out of the republic, which reached around 700,000 tons/year. During the first 5 months of 1999, Chechnya produced only 96,000 tons of oil. The drop in oil income largely contributed to the chaotic and anarchic situation in Chechnya in the late-1990s.

Besides oil, an important source of money was criminal activity, ranging from stealing federal aid to taking hostages for ransom and even slave trade. Drug trafficking also played an important role. Drugs were often being received as a form of "financial support" from the Taliban and were later sold in the Russian territory for cash. In 1998, the Chechens constituted 33 percent[90] among the ethnic groups in Russia most active in drug trafficking.

As the Chechen leadership was unable to maintain even the most basic forms of authority outside the city centers, Islamic radicals began establishing their own writ in rural, mountainous regions under the religious guidelines set by radical Islam and Sharia law. The Chechen "official" secessionist forces were under-funded, undermanned, and demoralized.

One partnership that helped to boost radical Islam in North Caucasus during this period was the rela-tionship between the Chechen guerilla commander and the emerging military leader of the Islamist move-ment Shamil Basayev, and a Salafi emissary and Saudi citizen known by the *nom de guerre,* Ibn al-Khattab.[91] The two developed a plan and launched a campaign to unite Chechnya with the North Caucasian republic of Dagestan to the east.[92] Many other radical Islamists from around the Middle East and the Balkans also flocked to Chechnya. Cornell notes how the Bosnian Islamists who emigrated from the Balkans after the implementation of the Dayton Accords found a new jihad theater for an Islamist Caliphate — this time in the mountains of the Caucasus.[93]

During the interwar period, "slave trade" in Chechnya flourished.[94] In fact, it was rather a market where hostages were bought and sold for ransom or in anticipation of such. This trade served as an important source of income for the separatists. The rebels did not limit the kidnappings to Chechnya, and victims were often smuggled in from neighboring Dagestan, as well as Moscow, Saint Petersburg, and other Russian cities. They would be held in Chechnya until ransom was received. In some cases, hostages were kept in the cities where they were captured, but this fact became known to the relatives only after they had paid the ransom.

One of the most prominent hostage takers and slave traders was Arbi Barayev. He was also among the cruelest terrorists.[95] Before joining the separatist movement in 1991, Barayev served in the local traffic police. In 1995, he became a leader of the self-defense militia in the village of Alkhan-Kala to later become the commander of the "special Islamic battalion" and a Chechen separatist general. As a slave trader, he is known for having taken hostage a group of NTV journalists in 1997, when this practice started becoming a common occurrence in Chechnya. He also started kidnapping rich Chechens, instead of Russian soldiers, which distinguished him from those who focused on victims from outside of Chechnya.[96] Barayev was, by far, not the only slave trader. Other known separatist leaders, such as Shamil Basayev, were also involved in hostage taking and slave trade.

In 2005, a Russian television channel NTV released a documentary called "Open-Hearted Confession — Prisoners of the Caucasus."[97] Based on interviews with former victims, this documentary describes the selection of victims, methods of blackmailing their relatives, and sizes of the ransoms. The slave traders did not kidnap random victims, but focused on wealthy individuals such as children of rich parents, journalists, and foreigners. After the hostages were captured, the process of blackmailing was similar to what we see in movies. The terrorists sent the relatives of the victim a videotape where he or she is begging them for help. As a sign that the terrorists should be taken seriously, they often cut their victims' fingers while capturing the entire scene on camera. If the ransom was not paid, the victims often spent up to a year (and sometimes even more) in captivity before, in many cases, being found and freed by the Russians. Most of the time the ransoms ranged from $3,000 to $20,000.[98] The NTV documentary mentions amounts as high as $70,000 in one case and allegedly as much as $500,000 in another. During the period of 1993–2005, 912 hostages were taken in Dagestan, of which 868 were successfully freed by the Russian forces. According to Vyacheslav Izmaylov, a war journalist, overall around 1,500 hostages were freed, but many more were taken.[99]

In 1996–99, Chechnya boasted a totally "legal" arms market, situated in the central Grozny marketplace. At this open-air suk, a Kalashnikov automatic could be bought for around $200–$300 and a Makarov pistol for around $600. A grenade cost 30 rubles.[100] However, weapons also were flowing in from abroad, and more importantly, they came with foreign instructors.

The radical Islamist recruiters found many Chechen recruits among the young war veterans and unemployed who found little hope in a brighter future in the de facto independent Chechen Republic of Ichkeria, where many converted to the Salafi-Wahhabi radical ideology. As the radicals attempt to deny and reject ethnic identity, the recruits reduced their allegiance to Chechen or other Caucasian ethnic identity—as do global Islamists operating from the Philippines and Thailand to Afghanistan to East Africa and the Magreb (North Africa). Much of the new radicalized forces congregated in southeastern Chechnya near the border with Dagestan and with the Republic of Georgia. They were strategically located in this area because it would be the staging zone for an invasion of Dagestan on August 7, 1999, in an attempt to unite

Chechnya and Dagestan into an Islamic Caliphate—
a religious-military dictatorship ruled by Sharia law.
Basayev and Ibn al-Khattab recruited the fighters
necessary to invade from the same area where they
established the "Islamic brigade."[101] However, war fa-
tigue after the previous conflict with Russia, rejection
of radicalization by large parts of the population, and
internal divisions within the Chechen government
would make fighting the Russians for the second time
far more difficult.[102]

THE SECOND CHECHNYAN WAR

When Yeltsin's handpicked successor, Vladimir
Putin, became Prime Minister in the summer of 1999,
he was a fierce proponent of forcibly bringing Chechnya under undisputed Russian control. This stance
secured him the support of the Russian military as
Putin solidified his power during the early period of
his presidency.

To justify their case for a war, Putin and his col-
leagues pointed out that the conflict in North Caucasus has evolved from an internal, separatist insurgency—in which the world mostly refrained from
interference or was sympathetic to the rebels—to a
struggle against radical Islamism, in which the world
should stand with Russia. In addition, Russia began
its public-relations campaign to convince its citizens
and foreign powers that Chechens and other Muslim
Caucasian terrorists were an existential threat to all
Russian civilians. Moscow started claiming, not without reason, that the conflict in the North Caucasus was
no longer a local fight for national liberation by the
"freedom-loving Chechens" but a terrorist threat to
Russians and other ethnic groups.[103]

Unlike the First Chechen War, in which Russia had made the first move, the Second Chechen War started in August 1999, after terrorist forces led by Shamil Basayev invaded Dagestan from Chechnya in an attempt to unite the two republics. The vision, articulated by al-Qaeda's number two, Ayman al-Zawahiri, was to connect Afghanistan with North Caucasus through a Caspian Sea "bridge." Putin and the Russian military responded with similar overwhelming force similar to that seen in the first war.[104] Devastation, displacement, and civilian deaths were again staggering.

Exact official data on civilian casualties during the Chechen wars are not available. Estimated numbers of victims are based mostly on assessments by nongovernmental organizations (NGOs), but the numbers vary considerably. A conservative estimate of the number of civilian casualties in Grozny alone during the first war is between 25,000 and 29,000.[105] Various Russian officials provided wide-ranging estimates of casualties. For instance, then Russian Interior Minister Anatoly Kulikov claimed that the number of civilians who lost their lives was below 20,000.[106] Conversely, Sergey Kovalyov's estimate is around 50,000, and General Aleksander Lebed spoke about 80,000–100,000 civilians killed. According to Taus Dzhabrailov, the head of the Chechnya National Council in the mid-2000s, 150,000 to 160,000 people are believed to have died as a result of both Chechen wars, out of whom 75,000 were Chechen civilians.[107]

After the start of the Second Chechen War, Maskhadov filed a suit against Kadyrov in the Sharia court for engaging in negotiations with Prime Minister Putin.[108] Kadyrov was sentenced to death and removed from the post of the Mufti.[109] This led Kadyrov to use his support from the Kremlin to hunt down

Maskhadov. During a special operation of the Russian Federal Security Service (FSB) in 2005, Maskhadov was allegedly shot dead by his bodyguard in order to avoid being taken prisoner.[110] Kadyrov himself left the post of the Mufti after he was appointed the new head of Chechnya in June 2000. In August 2000, Akhmathadji Shamayev was appointed the Mufti by a congress of the imams of Chechnya.[111]

During the Second Chechen War, Russian forces crushed the radical Islamic faction and retook control of Chechnya, thus ending its de facto independence. Many of the Chechen leaders were killed in battle. Former President Zelimkhan Yandarbiyev was assassinated on February 13, 2004, by a car explosion in Doha, Qatar. Two Russian diplomats were accused of his murder and sentenced to 25 years in a Qatari prison, but after serving 9 months they were transferred to Russia.[112] The Russian Ministry of Justice declined to disclose where they are serving the rest of their prison term, which suggests that they were silently released.[113] Maskhadov was killed on May 8, 2005, during a special operation of the FSB, and Basayev was killed on July 10, 2006, also during a Russian special operation.

In the Second Chechen War, Russia was much more effective in using ethnic Chechen units and intelligence sources against the separatists.[114] Many of them were rather opportunistic "pro-Russian" formations; nevertheless, they greatly contributed to the Russian victory. Their cooperation allowed Moscow to stop negotiating with the separatists and their leaders, and transform the conflict as a whole.

Information Warfare Aspect of the Conflict.

Russia's ability to use propaganda to change the perception of the war in the Caucasus proved crucial in helping it not only regain control of the region, but also convince Russian citizens and the international community that the policies toward the Caucasus were the right ones at the right time. This was in a striking contrast with the hapless course that brought about the defeat and the inglorious Khasavyurt accords of 1996. Information management became an important aspect of the conflict. Russia, with the help of government-controlled media (especially TV channels), tried to censor the war crimes committed by the security and military forces during and after the active phase of the conflict, and attempted to portray this war as a fight for Russian sovereignty. Russian media also spun the hostilities and the struggle between Chechen factions — the radical Islamists and terrorists — and the legitimate Chechen nationalists fighters led by the Kadyrovs.

The federal forces prepared for the Second Chechen War better than they did for the first one. While Basayev and his bands were still in Dagestan, the leadership of the federal forces chose a strategy which used artillery and bombing raids first, followed by infantry assaults.[115] This tactic turned out to be a success and led to relatively small losses among the Russian forces. Heavy Russian bombardment demoralized the rebels, and Basayev was forced to flee from Dagestan back to Chechnya. In Chechnya, the Russians tried to minimize the need for armed conflict. At first, they held talks with village elders and gave them a chance to persuade the rebels to voluntarily leave their villages. If the rebels agreed and if no one in the village opened fire on the federal forces, the Russians would not fire at the civilians.

The leadership of the federal forces anticipated that the rebels would leave the besieged Grozny voluntarily as well.[116] These expectations did not come true, and Russian military stormed Grozny. The air force conducted heavy aerial attacks using Su-24 and Su-25 fighters and helicopters. The pilots had to operate under air-defense missile fire from the Chechen radicals. Just as in the First Chechen War, the rebels used mainly Strela of various modifications, Igla, and some Stinger portable air defense systems.[117]

Similar to the first Chechen campaign, Russian soldiers taking Grozny in 1999–2000 were not sufficiently trained for urban warfare.[118] Besides poor preparation, the operations also suffered from flawed coordination between the Russian uniformed military and the country's internal troops under the Ministry of Interior, which also took part in the attack. After the Russians recaptured Grozny in 2000, the fighting moved deep into the Chechen territory. The rebels fled into their mountain bases located in caves, and the mountainous warfare made the situation more difficult for the Russians. The federal forces decided to engage attack planes and thermobaric (including fuel-air) weapons against the rebels hiding in the mountainous terrain.[119] The main thermobaric delivery system the Russians used in Grozny was the "Buratino" (TOS-1),[120] a system with a maximum effective range of 3.5 kilometers and a 200 x 400 meter zone of ensured destruction. Another thermobaric system reportedly used in Chechnya was a shoulder-launched rocket similar to RPG called RPO-A Schmel. This system has a maximum effective range of 600 meters, and a 50-square-meter zone of destruction in the open.

Indigenous political leadership was more important in Chechnya than the immediate military victory. Among the pro-Russian Chechen leaders was Mufti Ahmad Kadyrov, who formerly fought with Dudayev in the First Chechen War, but then clashed with Maskhadov. Kadyrov became the head of the pro-Moscow government in Grozny established after the end of formal hostilities in 2000. He had Moscow's blessing to do whatever was needed to maintain the supremacy of Russian rule in the republic. When the September 11, 2001 terrorist attacks gave credibility to Putin's policy toward the radicals in the Caucasus, Russia not only managed to regain control of lost territory in Chechnya but also, to some extent, win the propaganda war against the radicalized Chechen factions and foreign fighters.

Chechen rebels, who self-identified as Islamists (Salafis-Wahhabis), allowed Russia to utilize the traditional Sufi allegiance of the Chechens to build pro-Russian fighting forces, who had superior local knowledge and high level of motivation, rather than solely using the conventional Russian military. However, even though Russia declared the second war over in 2004, that year marked the beginning of the fight between Russia and the pro-Russian Chechen government against radical Islamists in the Northern Caucasus, with the hostilities expanding throughout the region and spilling over to all of Russia.

GROWTH OF TERRORIST ACTIVITY AND RADICALISM IN THE NORTHERN CAUCASUS SINCE THE SECOND CHECHEN WAR

The end of the active phase of the Second Chechen War in 2000 did not bring an end to modern political Islam and Islamist terrorism on the Russian territory. The terrorist factions that threaten Russia and have reached as far as Boston in 2013 have roots in the Chechen wars as well as in the global jihadi movement, as the Tsarnaev brothers' website demonstrated. In addition, global Islamist factions striving for seizure of political control in Muslim lands and eventual creation of the Califate, such as the Muslim Brotherhood and Hizb-ut-Tahrir al Islami (Islamic Army of Liberation), decided to commit more resources to Russia when they saw the successes of the Islamist fighters in North Caucasus.

Having been defeated on the battlefield, Basayev turned his attention to attacking soft targets outside Chechnya and Dagestan, not for any tactical gain against the Russian military but for the terroristic, traumatizing value of such acts. Meanwhile, within much of Chechnya and neighboring republics, radicals, domestic and foreign, began expanding the terrorist network by establishing Salafi *jamaats* (communities) throughout the region. They took advantage of the unique geography and the desperate socio-economic conditions that helped to recruit many young locals to commit to their radical movement. Many, therefore, joined the Islamist groups and moved away to isolated areas, escaping the authorities' writ and solidifying their commitment to increase their influence and plan attacks.[121]

Moreover, Islamist leaders like Basayev and, later, Doku Umarov, began outlining jihadist manifestos that definitively declared their desire to transform North Caucasus into a Caliphate and a vehicle of the pan-Islamist fundamentalist force fighting against Russians not just for independence but for global jihad.[122] The radicals began with the implementation of Sharia law throughout the former Chechen Republic of Ichkeria and in the Salafi *jamaats*, over which their followers had influence outside of Chechnya. After Dudayev was killed and Zelimkhan Yandarbiyev became acting president of Ichkeria in April 1996, the process accelerated.[123]

As in other Muslim societies, Sharia law is perceived as God-given and thus paramount over laws or doctrines coming from civil or common law systems, such as parliamentary legislation and precedent-based law. According to the traditionalist interpretations of the *Koran* and other Islamic holy scriptures, Sharia law is not open to interpretation or amendment by secular scholars. This legal doctrine contrasts with the traditional Chechen and Caucasian attitudes toward Islam, as many in the region are devout Muslims, but have preferred to follow Sufi Islam, which accepts the following of Sufi saints and cultural icons that make up the separate religious and cultural identities of the Caucasian peoples.[124] The radicals, on the other hand, adhere to the militant monotheistic principle of *tawhid* in which the worshiping or praying to any entity besides Allah—even to Muhammad himself —is sacrilegious.[125] Throughout the world, Salafi followers of the *tawhid* often destroy graves of venerated saints, forbid any local worship, including that of ancestors, and are generally much more intolerant than the Sufis. Having established Sharia law, the radicals needed to implement doctrines in order to "purify" the region from *kafirs* (infidels), who do not practice Islam in accordance to their dogma.

After the assassination of Basayev in 2006 by the Russian Special Forces, the new head of the Caucasus-based Islamist movement, Doku Umarov, established the Caucasus Emirate (*Imarat Kavkaz*, or CE) based on Sharia law and with goals consistent with fundamentalist Wahabbist-Salafist teachings of Islam.[126] This restatement of Umarov's militant Islamist ideology is important to understand the radical direction in which the North Caucasus insurgency is moving.

CE's initial manifesto declared its objective to unite all of the Northern Caucasus into a single "Caucasus Emirate," eliminating all the borders separating autonomous republics and all ethnic, linguistic, and cultural distinctions as un-Islamic. The whole region was supposed to become one frontline of the global jihad in the name of Allah and against the infidels. In order to achieve this goal, the Islamists needed to force Russia to relinquish its control over the region, as has been the demand among separatists for centuries. The extremists also seek to force the various republics and ethnic groups to renounce any indigenous identity, that has been cherished and valued, and submit completely to radical Islamist ideology and command, including the "Amir" Umarov, and join global jihad. Once achieving total control, Umarov and CE would begin to spread their war to the Muslim areas in the Urals, Central Asia, and Siberia, with future plans to conquer all of Russia, including Moscow.[127]

The CE became an Islamist affiliate of the global al-Qaeda-led movement that operated symbiotically with terrorist cells all across the Middle East and Eurasia. CE and other Northern Caucasus radicals received tactical, financial, and moral support from al-Qaeda and its partners.[128] For example, Caucasian terrorists benefited from the expertise of al-Qaeda operatives Muhammad al Emirati and Abdulla Kurd, who helped organize operational activities within the region while coordinating with al-Qaeda globally. Though Russian counterterrorist forces killed both of them in April 2011, they advanced CE's mission to connect with global jihad.[129] Beyond this relationship, al-Qaeda's tentacles in the region go back to the 1990s, even before the paradigm of Caucasian rebellion against Russia changed to jihadist. Hahn documents the many instances of al-Qaeda contributing arms, funds, Islamist education, and access to training camps in Afghanistan and elsewhere, for fighters from the Chechen Republic of Ichkeria. Al-Qaeda's Ayman al-Zawahiri once stated that the North Caucasus represented "one of three primary fronts in the war against the West," and CE's actions attempted to match his rhetoric.[130]

The Second Terror Campaign.

With the help of foreign jihadi organizations and the infusion of new recruits and radical immigrants from the Balkans, the year 2000 marked the beginning of a new Islamist terrorist campaign against the Russian population, striking targets as far as Moscow. This was a startling development in comparison with the wars between Russia and Chechnya, as conflicts had remained contained within the Caucasus. The first known case of terrorism as a tactical as well as a psychological weapon was during the First Chechen War in 1995, when Basayev executed a large suicide bombing of Russian forces in Chechnya.

Coinciding with the beginning of the second Chechen war, however, Chechen Islamist fighters led by Basayev focused on attacking Russian civilians. The earliest major attack was the 2002 Dubrovka Theater siege in Moscow in which 912 people were taken hostage.[131] Russian forces killed all the terrorists, but around 130 hostages perished with the terrorists. This Russian anti-terrorist operation is considered by many to be a failure of the special services. In 2006, the survivors and relatives of the victims prepared a 200-page report called "Nord-Ost—An Unfinished Investigation," in which they claim that the special services did not do everything they could to save as many people as possible, and accused them of negligence.[132] The most controversial aspect of the operation was the usage of a new type of nerve gas, which is believed to be responsible for the deaths of the terrorists and the 130 hostages. It appears that the authorities did not deploy medical teams near the Dubrovka Theater, amass ambulances before storming the target, or brief the medical personnel on the nerve agent use and ways to treat the patients. While hardly a surprise, given the poor state of Russian military medicine and the health system in general, this was a failure of emergency medicine of enormous proportions.

There have been numerous demands to release the information about the gas, the composition of which continues to remain secret.[133] However, Aleksey Filatov, a former Alpha special forces unit fighter, justified using the gas by claiming that, because the gas was used, the terrorists failed to detonate the bomb they had with them, in which case the number of casualties would have significantly exceeded the number of those killed by the gas.[134]

Several years earlier in September 1999, a series of apartment bombings shattered the peace in Russia.[135] Four apartment buildings were blown up in cities across Russia: two of them in Moscow, one in Buynaksk (Dagestan), and one in Volgodonsk (Rostovskaya Oblast'). Around 300 people lost their lives, and many more were wounded. The terrorist attacks are believed to have been committed by separatists from North Caucasus as an act of revenge for Moscow's military operations in Chechnya and Dagestan. There are many, however, who challenge the veracity of this version of events.

Since the beginning of the 21st century, Basayev and Umarov perpetrated a series of terrorist attacks across Russia. The most notable examples are the attacks on a school in Beslan in 2004, the Saint Petersburg-Moscow passenger train in late-2009, the Moscow metro in 2010, and on Domodedovo Airport in Moscow in January 2011. The U.S. Department of State and the United Nations (UN) recognized these attacks as committed by Chechen terrorists, seeking to establish the Caucasus Emirate.[136]

On September 1, 2004, a group of 17 terrorists took around 1,100-1,400 people hostage in an elementary school in the town of Beslan in North Ossetia.[137] The FSB-led operation to release the hostages remains controversial. On September 3, the FSB forces undertook a counterattack, which resulted in a chaotic exchange of fire between them and the terrorists.[138] The efforts of the FSB and the supporting troops suffered from a lack of coordination and were further complicated by many armed civilians voluntarily trying to help free the hostages. One of the reasons for the poor coordination is allegedly the fact that the FSB forces expected only 354 hostages to be in the school, which resulted in choosing a wrong strategy for the attack.[139] Also, they did not set a perimeter, which initially prevented FSB forces from sealing the school and later allowed some of the terrorists to escape. As a result of the operation, 335 hostages were killed. How many hostages died at the hands of the terrorists, how many as a result of the FSB using heavy weaponry, and how many due to the mistakes of the rescue team remains unclear.[140] If the Russian military and security forces conducted a "lessons learned" investigation, it remains hidden from the public.

In the Northern Caucasus, CE and other radicals continued their guerrilla war against Russian forces at a staggering pace that earned Russia the dubious distinction of having one of the highest rates of terrorist attacks per year in the world.[141] In effect, over the past decade, the North Caucasus has become an ungovernable area and a part of the global jihad space. Local Islamist organizations are now capable of launching their own operations with some level of cooperation with global terrorist networks, as arrests in Europe and the Boston attack have demonstrated. More intelligence activities will be necessary to better understand the multiple facets of this cooperation.

Russian Counterterrorism and Counterinsurgency in the 21st Century.

Russia's porous borders and insufficient surveillance throughout the region; inadequate local knowledge of the counterintelligence forces assigned to North Caucasus from around the country; a lack of linguistic skills by the regular military as well as special forces; and corruption of the local authorities and economic development programs severely affected

Russian anti-terrorist and counterinsurgency responses. North Caucasus, in addition to terrorism and
Islamism, has become a hotspot of drug and human
trafficking that further funded terrorist activities and
solidified the relationships between the Caucasus and
drug havens of Afghanistan and Tajikistan and other
global trafficking networks. Chechen and other North
Caucasus networks have become significant narcot-
ics distribution platforms for Russia and Eastern and
Western Europe.

Doku Umarov's Caucasian Emirate has become a
formidable coalition of various decentralized *jamaats*
that, despite Russian efforts so far, has avoided having its network substantially exposed and liquidated.
Just like Islamist radicals elsewhere, CE members have
successfully hidden from scrutiny and entrenched
themselves in order to continue operations. They have
managed to transform much of their historic grand
strategy of regional guerilla warfare aimed at achieving independence from Russia — into one that includes
underground tactics and urban warfare, while invok-
ing radical ideology that had little connection with the
history of the region. However, given the enormity
of the international jihadi goals, it is too early to tell
whether CE will manage to achieve its objectives do-
mestically and regionally, and whether its comrades-
in-arms would succeed globally.

RUSSIAN COUNTERTERRORIST
AND COUNTERINSURGENCY RESPONSES
AND STRATEGIES SINCE 2000

After the successful recapture of Dagestan and
Chechnya by Russia in 2000, Russian military and interior ministry units in North Caucasus have become

primarily a counterterrorist force. However, they lack appropriate training, equipment, and motivation. With Putin ascending to the presidency in the same year, Russian counterterrorist operations maintained "search and destroy" tactics to stop the growth of radical Islam in the Northern Caucasus. Yet, since 2000, Moscow and Grozny have not fully eliminated the terrorist threat in the North Caucasus. As Sergey Markedonov from the Center for Strategic and International Studies (CSIS) notes, the main failure of the Russian counterinsurgency in the North Caucasus was the absence of a relevant, well thought out and coherently implemented strategy. Practically all operations, even the successful ones, look like belated responses.

Another problem is the correct identification of the enemy. Russian officials, including at the highest level, tend to refer to the separatists as terrorists or "bandits."[142] However, terrorism is not criminal activity; it is political violence, Markedonov says.[143] Thus it is necessary to understand the ideological roots of the current Caucasian terrorists and their political goals. Since the late-1990s, terrorism under nationalist and self-determination slogans has been replaced by an Islamic one. However, even today Russian officials continue to speak about the "Chechen separatists."[144]

Meanwhile, the situation in the North Caucasus no longer resembles the dynamics of the Chechen conflict. The insurgency in the region is not centered in Chechnya anymore. Rather, every year since 2005, the recorded incidence of violence in Chechnya has been less than, or equal to, the levels of violence observed in the neighboring republics of Ingushetia and Dagestan. Ideologically, the Russian government does not propose any attractive alternatives to militant Islam. Instead, it is restricting its policy by supporting the state-sponsored Spiritual Board of Muslims (*Dukhovnye Upravleniya Musul'man,* or DUMs), while underestimating the role of unofficial Muslims who are not subordinated to DUMs and not engaged in the terrorist activity and jihadist propaganda.

Russian intelligence, counterterrorism, and strategic communities at times developed and implemented policies that were actually causing radical Islam to grow in the region. Outside their military and intelligence networks, Moscow has mainly relied on the subsidiary government in Chechnya led by, first, Mufti Ahmad Kadyrov, and after his death in the bombing during the celebration of the Russian V-E day on May 9, 2004, by his son, Ramzan.[145] Kadyrov the younger managed to bring the violence in the republic under control. However, he has a dubious human rights record, ranging from alleged killings of prominent Russian journalists who openly criticized his practices, to hunting down and killing his opponents abroad. A notable case of such killing is the assassination of Umar Israilov in Vienna, Austria, on January 30, 2009.[146] Israilov was a former bodyguard of Kadyrov, but later turned into an open critic of Kadyrov's regime in Chechnya and fled to Austria, where he was given asylum.

The dynamics of Chechen society have, so far, worked to Kadyrov and Moscow's advantage, because most of the Chechens still want to identify as being loyal to the Vaynach (Chechen) nation, rather than to adopt radical Islam and erase their discrete identity. Kadyrov has had a great impact on local society through repression of terrorist activity and promoting the "Chechen national identity," which coexists and complements, not supplants, religious practices.

Through Chechen efforts and Russian subsidies, Grozny and other cities underwent massive post-war reconstruction and development that included constructing the Grozny Central Mosque, the largest mosque in Europe, Russia, and Eurasia, and one of the largest in the world, apparently with Turkish funding.[147] This was done in order to further develop Chechen culture and traditional Sufi Islam and as an attempt to supplant the appeal of radical, global Islam.[148]

In what could be seen as an improvement in Russian-Chechen relations, the promotion of Chechen culture by the Kadyrov regime after the Second Chechen War is one of the few policy planks on which Russian and Chechen leaderships have actively collaborated. In order to further promote the government's version of Chechen society over the radical ideology and to increase his own popularity, Kadyrov legalized polygamy (even though it is illegal under Russian law and the constitution).[149] What Kadyrov did in the hope of improving the situation in Chechnya and decreasing the influence of radical Islamists in the area, with the blessing from Moscow, appears to have been more effective than Moscow's actions.[150]

The fact that the current Russian counterinsurgency strategy is far from being fully successful is demonstrated by many news accounts detailing the ongoing violence in the region. As recently as June 23, 2013, 38 special police officers were killed in clashes in southwestern Chechnya.[151] Another two police officers were killed in the Shatoy district on June 29.

Aleksey Malashenko, co-chair of the Carnegie Moscow Center's Religion, Society, and Security Program, believes that the Kremlin did not learn any political lessons from the two Chechen campaigns.[152] He notes that "the Kremlin has no productive strategy in North Caucasus; its policy toward the region is mostly reactive." Another drawback of the policy of the Kremlin, Malashenko believes, is that it is not able to prevent the emergence of a new generation of mujahedeen. Effective measures against their rise would inevitably have to include a dialogue with the opposition and undertaking practical measures to combat the ubiquitous corruption in the region—something that the current elites are unwilling and unlikely to do.[153]

International Criticism of Russia and the Kadyrov Government.

International observers from the UN, OSCE, the United States, and from human rights organizations, have criticized the Government of Russia and Kadyrov's Chechen Republic for anti-terrorist activities that violate human rights and the laws of war. The U.S. Congress has stated that Chechen governmental forces are emulating the abusive tactics of the terrorists.[154] The United States is under pressure to freeze Kadyrov's bank accounts in response to these condemnations.[155] Reportedly, Kadyrov's name is in the classified section of the Magnitsky List, the U.S. law named after a Russian anti-corruption whistle blower who died in a Moscow prison awaiting trial, and that targets gross violators of human rights.[156] However, despite the overwhelming use of force, many in Chechnya seem to have accepted the Kadyrov rule as "the lesser of two evils" between the available options, despite the fact that Kadyrov apparently has violated many Russian laws and may be guilty of serious crimes.

For now, Chechnya is no longer in an all-out war with Russia. Despite high unemployment, it is emerging from a debilitating economic depression. As long as Kadyrov maintains this modicum of security and income for the population, the Chechens will not risk altering the situation radically by combating Russia or swelling the ranks of the Islamists. They live with Putin and Kadyrov for now — but as in the past, this may change quickly.[157]

Russia, for its part, uses conventional, counterterrorist forces and soft-power means like economic aid, subsidies, and development schemes in order to help sustain a pro-Moscow government facing an Islamist threat. With the Kadyrov government becoming more entrenched, Putin's Kremlin has been willing to live with a manufactured Chechen-nationalist narrative that uses Chechen history and tradition in order to simulate a "rebirth" of Chechen national pride; however, this "renaissance" has become more of a make-shift 21st-century post-modern artifact sustained and regulated by Grozny and Moscow. For now, it has been effective in striking a balance between de facto independence short of the trappings of sovereignty, such as full border control, foreign relations, and formally independent armed forces. Moscow and Grozny, too, consider this the lesser of two evils.

Yet, the renaissance comes at a price. There are reports that Kadyrov is allowed to control a good portion of the lucrative real estate market in Moscow. This combination of strong-arm tactics, lucrative business ventures, and criminality helps to keep the Kadyrov regime under Kremlin's control, while maintaining Moscow's domination over the region by being Kadyrov's de facto banker and protector. Thanks to Moscow's strategic financial injections, Kadyrov has overseen the rebuilding and development of city blocks, shopping centers, and other major construction projects, including support of the faith. In order to promote further the "state-compatible" form of Islam, Kadyrov has been financing Chechens' flights to Mecca for Hajj, one of the five obligatory Islamic pillars of faith.[158]

One of the reasons why the Chechen people continue to join the insurgency and become followers of radical Islamic ideologies is the long-term lack of opportunities and gloomy prospects for the future. Despite the heavy financial support from the Russian federal budget, Chechnya is the second poorest subject of the Russian Federation in terms of gross domestic product (GDP) per capita after Ingushetia, with approximate GDP per capita of $1,850 in 2010.[159] Chechnya has levels of unemployment that are unsustainably high for a self-sufficient economy. The official unemployment level in late-2012 was 25.3 percent.[160] However, according to Russian media sources, the real Chechen unemployment is as high as 70 percent, with youth unemployment being even higher.[161] The high unemployment rates and low salaries of those who are lucky enough to be employed reflect the lack of prospects and opportunities, especially for young people. One may think that with over 90 percent of Chechnya's budget bankrolled by Moscow, Kadyrov's government can only create and execute policy that has the blessing from the Kremlin in order to preserve the still tenuous tranquility.[162] However, Moscow itself is a hostage of sorts in Chechnya, as no one today is seen as capable of replacing Kadyrov.

Meanwhile, Chechen refugees in Europe are gradually organizing themselves and forming a well-established diaspora. The largest Chechen diaspora is in

Western European countries, such as Norway, France, Belgium, Germany, and Austria, and made up of an estimated 10,000 to 30,000 people in each of those countries.[163] *The Caucasus Times* claims that this newly formed Chechen diaspora is able to exert influence on the situation in Chechnya.[164]

There are several organizations in the Chechen diaspora. For instance, the World Chechen Congress is registered as an NGO in Belgium.[165] Another organization is the Chechen Diaspora of Norway.[166] Additionally, in September 2010, a "virtual" World Chechen Congress took place in Poland, which was a controversial event evoking negative reactions among anti-Kremlin Chechens.[167] For instance, Zhalodi Saralyapov, speaker of the so-called Parliament of the "Chechen Republic of Ichkeria," said that these actions "are aimed at destabilizing the situation in the Chechen national liberation movement, at the destruction of positive developments acquired during the long war."[168] Members of the Chechen diaspora in countries all across Europe distanced themselves from the congress, stating that it was organized by Russians in order to consolidate the Russian occupation of Chechnya.

The members of the Chechen diaspora are not united. A majority of Chechen refugees may be supportive of the Islamist outlook, saying that they want to see the fight for independence continue (66 percent) and that they have a positive attitude toward establishing a single North Caucasus republic (54 percent). There is also a small group who are pro-Kadyrov in their views.[169] These people actively promote the ideas of a common state with Russia.

Under the Dmitry Medvedev administration (2009-12), in order to promote a "softer" approach to exerting Moscow's power over the region, the Kremlin has created the Northern-Caucasian Federal District and Northern-Caucasian Economic District. Alexander Khloponin, the Kremlin-appointed "Governor-General" of the Northern-Caucasian Federal District, has outlined the District's broad goals and individual projects. Khloponin announced that by 2020 the region will be part of a transportation network that will link the North Caucasus with the rest of Russia, the Middle East, and Central Asia. He has proposed various projects, including road infrastructure, building holiday resorts, improving regional access to higher education, making airport renovations, and constructing hydroelectric plants across the entire North Caucasus.[170] Recent investigations of the resorts scheme suggest that a good part of these projects were means to illicitly syphon off budgetary funds into the private pockets of "favored" businessmen who are particularly close to the powers that be.[171]

The same can be alleged about the Sochi Winter Olympics in 2014. The Russian Ministry of Regional Development announced in 2010 (almost 4 years before the games) that the expenses for preparing for the Olympics had already surpassed $30 billion.[172] Other sources claim that the Sochi "subtropical" Winter Olympics will cost $50 billion. In comparison, the cost of the last Winter Olympics in Vancouver in 2010 is estimated to have been between $3.6 and $6 billion.[173] According to Boris Nemtsov, the former Russian First Deputy Prime Minister and a leader of the Russian opposition banned from the Duma, the overall amount of embezzlement at the Sochi Olympics has already reached about $25–$30 billion.[174] He believes that the total expenditures have already surpassed $50 billion, which makes it the most expensive Winter Olympics in human history.

The responsibility of national security, however, for Northern Caucasus, is a partnership between the autonomous republic governments and the federal, Moscow-based national security institutions. The national security apparatus within the federal government has indeed maintained the lead in intelligence, reconnaissance, and support for what Putin tries to portray as a solely "regional problem," but which in reality threatens the whole of Russia and beyond.

In 2006, Russia established the National Anti-Terrorism Committee, headed ex-officio by the Director of the FSB, in order to bring various departments in one silo, where counterterrorist policy could be better formulated and implemented more efficiently.[175] Even with better coordination, however, violence and death are still rampant throughout the North Caucasus. Pummeled by hostile media and public opinion, Doku Umarov, the CE emir, has made a declaration on behalf of CE in 2012 that terrorists under his command would "stop attacks against Russian civilians" and, instead, focus their efforts on battling military, police, government officials, or the security apparatus.[176] The sincerity of Umarov's declaration remains uncertain: the statement may have been made just to get better public relations, or in order to cajole Russians into moderating their assaults on CE and its terrorist networks. His public affairs track record remains, unsurprisingly, spotty: in fact, Umarov allegedly announced his resignation on August 1, 2010, due to poor health.[177] The next day, however, Umarov released another video where he called his former announcement faked.[178] He also said that he was in good health.

In fact, Umarov had assumed a less active role in CE but retains the top leadership position in the group, which signifies how decentralized the command structure in this terrorist network is, in sync with other net-centric terrorist organizations around the world.[179] Rogue actors in the North Caucasus, real or imagined, still attack civilians, defying Umarov's declaration. Moreover, the events in Belgium and Boston, where North Caucasus terrorists were arrested, demonstrate that the world must not discount the threat of Islamic radicalism in the North Caucasus to European and American national security.

EFFECT OF NORTHERN CAUCASUS ON BROADER RUSSIAN, AMERICAN, AND GLOBAL SECURITY

With Islamist terrorist activities challenging Russia's control in the North Caucasus, Moscow risks having the insurgency undermine Russian strategic goals of reestablishing itself as a leading global power. With the advent of the 2014 Winter Olympic Games and the 2018 Soccer World Cup in Russia, Putin and the ruling elite are eager to use these and other Russian-hosted global events to improve the country's image, attract global investment, and secure the world's confidence that Russia is a 21st-century global leader akin to China, India, and Brazil. If one of those events were to attacked, the consequences for Russia's global image would be extremely negative. While Umarov pledged to attack Sochi in 2014, Putin has managed to convince much of the world that the security problems in the North Caucasus, in spite of sporadic attacks and active terrorist cells, have been largely resolved.

The Long–term Rise in Radicalism.

Even though Russia made it through the Sochi Olympics with no casualties, the fight is far from over. Other regions in the Northern Caucasus, especially Dagestan, are experiencing a rise in Islamic radicalism. The origins of contemporary Islamic radicalism in Dagestan go back to the early-1990s, when the Soviet Union was collapsing and opening its borders to the outside world.[180] A key figure in organizing the radical Islamist movement in Dagestan was Bagauddin Kebedov. He was a devout supporter of Salafism and harshly criticized other, more moderate forms of Islam, such as Sufism. In 1990, he became one of the leaders of the Islamic Party of Revival and subsequently a leader of a radical wing of Dagestani Salafists, later named the Islamic Jamaat of Dagestan (IJD). The Salafi ideology enjoyed wide support among the population due to the deepening economic crisis, the simplicity and understandability of the Salafi ideas, and the spirit of brotherhood in the organization. The IJD gradually became the most influential Salafi group in Dagestan.

The protracted conflict in Chechnya was also one of the reasons that facilitated the spreading of this radical ideology in Dagestan. The 1996 withdrawal from Chechnya was a sign of Russian military weakness. It encouraged the Dagestani radicals to form closer ties with their brothers in faith. Many of them went to fight in Chechnya or joined local terrorist organizations. In addition, the Chechen conflict encouraged people who saw the war as a source of income to join the radicals.

The antigovernment and anti-Russian sentiments among the members of the IJD were encouraged by the counterproductive policy of local Dagestani authorities. They lacked a cohesive strategy to contain the IJD and instead chose to irritate it with police action. In particular, the local Dagestani authorities decided to launch what they considered to be a "total war" against the radical extremist groups. However, the ranks of Wahhabists were often filled by ordinary Muslims with no previous ties to extremists. Moreover, the "hunt on Wahhabists" was frequently used as a means to solve personal and political disputes, and also for the personal benefits of corrupt law enforcement and petty politicians. Using excessively harsh methods only motivated many Islamist activists to seek revenge or to go fight in Chechnya.

In 2012, the situation in Dagestan became critical.[181] Around three-quarters of all terrorist acts committed in the North Caucasus for the first 9 months of 2012 took place in Dagestan. Despite the minimal chances for success of their goal to establish an Islamic quasi-state, the Salafists/Wahhabists enjoy considerable support of the Dagestani population. Similarly to the early-1990s, people continue to be dissatisfied with an untenable economic situation, including unemployment, corruption, poor healthcare, and the lack of future prospects. However, the religious yearning and its violent manifestation also attract Dagestanis into the ranks of terrorists.

The situation in Ingushetia is similar to that in Dagestan. The influence of Islamic radicals in Ingushetia remains high despite the regular killing and capturing of radical terrorists and field commanders.[182] Salafi/Wahhabi ideology and organizations have a strong potential for the same reasons as in Dagestan. Moscow declared the counterterrorist operation in Chechnya completed in 2009. However, this action allowed terrorist activity to spread more easily to the neighboring republics, including Ingushetia.[183] Terrorist attacks continue to take place. The ranks of Wahhabists continue to be filled mainly by Ingushetia's youth who do not see other ways of self-realization.

Similarly, in Kabardino-Balkaria, the nationalism of the local ethnic communities dominates over civil values.[184] However, radical Islamist terrorists are active in Kabardino-Balkaria. For instance, on January 6, 2013, three suspected terrorists were killed by the Russian security services.[185] They are believed to have been preparing terrorist attacks against local churches during the celebration of the Orthodox Christmas. At least since 2009, the clashes between the rebels and the Russian security services in the republic have been a weekly, if not a more frequent, occurrence.[186] There are also reports that hundreds of Sunni fighters have joined radical forces in Syria to fight the Alawi regime of President Bashar el-Assad and his Shia allies, such as Hezbollah and Iran.[187] Russia no doubt applauds the exodus of the troublemakers, despite its support of the Assad regime: if killed or wounded in Syria, these extremists are "off the streets" in the Caucasus.

Nevertheless, the Russian experts interviewed in the course of this research agree that expectations of a general massive uprising in the North Caucasus against Moscow's rule are not realistic. Local uprisings are possible in the event that local administrations commit political mistakes, giving the insurgents an excuse to organize and act against the Kremlin.[188] In addition, there are numerous disputes within the region itself, such as interethnic tensions between the Ossetians and the Ingush or land disputes between different groups in Dagestan and Kabardino-Balkaria, let alone inter-republican border disputes (e.g., between North Ossetia and Ingushetia, and between Ingushetia and Chechnya).[189] Other examples of tensions include intra-Islamic disputes, such as those between Sufi Muslims, who consider their tribal lands to be a part of their ethno-national heritage, and the ultra-religious Salafis, who exhibit higher differing levels of radicalism, and violent followers of global jihad.

The partial remedy to deprive the rebels of an excuse to lure new mujahedeen seems to be economic and social development of the region; attractive secular policies; and the presence of a strong alternative to the radical brand of Islam. If corruption and unemployment are successfully dealt with and if the youth is given a viable and attractive alternative, the rebel leaders will lose their appeal, and the whole insurgency movement may gradually fade.

Instead, Moscow is trying to discredit radical Islamism as something that is foreign to "traditional Islam" and Caucasian ethnic traditions — a strategy that has so far had little effect. Paradoxically, this strategy has been unsuccessful despite the fact that even unofficial Muslims, not subordinated to the state-sponsored Islamic structures, are rather critical and suspicious of the "Caucasus Emirate" activity.[190] The local population in many cases fails to view federal institutions in the region as legitimate. In the meantime, the North Caucasus is gradually turning into a *de facto* "inner abroad" for Moscow.

In order for Moscow to achieve successes in fighting the North Caucasian separatists, its policy needs to include measures aimed at integrating at least some of the radicals into the Russian society. In other words, the resolve of the Kremlin to neutralize the separatists at all costs needs to be combined with "soft power" addressed to the citizens.[191] Russia needs to be able to distinguish a terrorist act from a gangland slaying (very often the highest representatives of the Russian state identify terrorists as "bandits"). These measures must be accompanied by a relentless anticorruption strategy (because "privatization" of the local power provokes social protest and radicalism), creation of new personnel for the republican level of public service — (well-educated beyond the Caucasian republics) — and promotion of alternative versions of Islam (regional Caucasus or European Islam for example).

Beyond the North Caucasus, the situation is slowly deteriorating. In particular, the Muslim-majority republics of Bashkortostan and Tatarstan, which are located in the core of Russia and far away from the North Caucasus, have started to develop Islamist networks that are linked with the Northern Caucasus and global networks. On July 19, 2012, Deputy Mufti Valiulla Yakupov was killed, and Ildus Fayzov, the Mufti of Tatarstan, was severely injured in a car bombing in Kazan, Tatarstan.[192] These clergymen were openly critical of the spread of Wahhabism in the country.[193] Radicalized citizens of Tatarstan have also been gone to fight in Chechnya and with the Taliban in Afghanistan.[194] Also, in Bashkortostan in February 2011, Bashkir officials stated that four Islamist radicals operating at the behest of Umarov were caught with a "homemade bomb" with the intention of inflicting mass civilian casualties.[195]

Since North Caucasus is an energy hub adjacent to the Black and Caspian Seas, the sabotage of energy infrastructure remains a constant concern among Russian energy firms upstream and downstream. As Russia strives to connect new pipelines like South Stream from Novorossiysk on the Black Sea to Turkey and Europe and continues to build up Krasnodar Krai's ports as energy-logistics hubs, Islamist terrorists in the North Caucasus will continue to focus on any opportunity to strike Russian energy trade and civilian population in a devastating way.

For the United States, the winding down of operations in Afghanistan and Iraq will change the U.S. focus on Central Asia and the Caucasus and its threat assessment of North Caucasus terrorism. After the withdrawal of the U.S. troops from Afghanistan in 2014, the country will most likely slip back into chaos, threatening the stability of the countries of Central Asia and North Caucasus, which has traditional political, religious, and drug-trafficking ties with Afghanistan's Taliban. Thus, the United States may be required to refocus on the region, which has so far received insufficient attention under the Barack Obama administration.

Terrorist networks from Russia will find new opportunities to undermine Russian and U.S. allies and the peace that the United States fought so hard to secure. Past reports show that Russian citizens from the Northern Caucasus have been active in combat and in drug trafficking in Afghanistan and South Asia.[196] North Caucasus terrorists also greatly benefited from the drug trade originating from Afghanistan.[197]

After the U.S. withdrawal from Afghanistan, the old ties are likely to revive. The global financing of terrorism is vital to help grow the North Caucasus Islamist network. The radical Islamists in the North Caucasus continue to challenge Russian federal authorities, thanks to the availability of outside sources of financing. As far back as 2000, Khattab and websites supportive of al-Qaeda have solicited financial support for North Caucasus groups, even before CE was established.[198] Through the global "charity" called Benevolence International Foundation, set up in Saudi Arabia, Chechen groups received vast amounts of money from the Middle East, before the international terrorism finance arm was shut down in Russia, the United

States, and elsewhere.[199] In 2010, a charity known as "Sharia4Belgium," which was sending money to CE, was thwarted, as well as numerous websites based in Europe that solicited and laundered funds that ultimately reached Islamic terrorist groups.[200]

Not only fraudulent "charities" in Europe were exposed as money-laundering schemes for terrorists; some North Caucasus cells have been uncovered in Europe as well. In the Czech Republic, a cell associated with CE, containing one Chechen and a couple of Dagestanis, among other Islamic radicals from Eastern Europe, was apprehended in April 2011. The French police found five Chechen nationals, including an imam, in a cell which made and stored components for making bombs.[201] Based on the nature of these findings, North Caucasus terrorism in Europe appears to target civilians and government officials regardless of what declaration Umarov might produce.

Finally, as already mentioned, Chechens and other extremist Sunni fighters from the North Caucasus have made their way via Turkey to Syria fighting for the Sunni rebels against the Alawi Assad regime. Hundreds of Islamists from the North Caucasus, notably Chechnya, have joined the rebellion against Syrian president Bashar al-Assad, even as Kadyrov states no Chechens are actively engaged in Syria.[202] A senior Azerbaijani official who requested anonymity estimated the number of North Caucasians fighting in Syria against Assad to be in the "hundreds." He complained that Russia is not doing much to stop the migration of its young men to fight a jihad in Syria because Russian authorities prefer "their" extremists to be killed far away from its borders.[203] On the other hand, if trained and battle-hardened in Syria, these fighters may come home and cause a lot of trouble to the pro-

Moscow administrations of their homeland. As seen in Europe, Syria, Afghanistan, and in North America (Boston), the North Caucasian threat is already global in nature, and active cooperation among international intelligence and law enforcement organizations is required in order to prevent this region from inflicting any more harm to American and international interests.

OUTLOOK AND RECOMMENDATIONS

While Kadyrov and Putin continue to eviscerate terrorists, their networks, and supporters, Russian society as a whole has made little progress in establishing an interethnic harmony and inter-religious détente between the ethnic Russian Orthodox majority and the Muslim North Caucasian peoples throughout the country. The Russian elites and Slavic Orthodox majority's attitudes toward the Caucasus vary. Some believe that Russia needs to stop pouring multibillion dollar subsidies from the federal budget to the likes of Kadyrov and to other Caucasus autonomous republics. Hence the famous slogan formulated by the opposition leader, Alexei Navalny: "Enough feeding the Caucasus."

Eventually, ethno-religious enmity and economic disparity may lead to political independence of the regions or parts thereof. Many prominent establishment figures, such as the former Prime Minister Yevgeny Primakov, Chairman of the Accounts Chamber of Russia and former Prime Minister Sergei Stepashin, the head of Rosatom and the former Prime Minister Sergey Kiriyenko, and the former Moscow mayor Yury Luzhkov, essentially agree that Russia should abandon the North Caucasus and build a new border on the Terek River. Yet, others still consider the Caucasus to be an aggravating problem that should be suppressed rather than resolved. Whichever the approach, Russia is unlikely to give up the North Caucasus unless forced to by the aforementioned factors.

The nationalist movements that have conspicuously expressed their animosity toward the region have pled to Putin to stop the government's assistance to governments in the Northern Caucasus at the expense of Slavic/Orthodox Russians. In the last few years, Russians have protested and rioted against the development aid to the Caucasus, as well as in response to alleged and real attacks on ethnic Russians by Caucasian migrants in cities and villages all across Russia. Locations included the village of Bezopasnoye (whose name ironically means "safe"), in Stavropolskaya Oblast'; Mirny, in Ulyanovsk oblast (which equally ironically means "peaceful"), the cosmopolitan capitals of Moscow and Saint-Petersburg;[204] Kondapoga in the Karelia, Pugachev (Saratov oblast');[205] Nizhny Novgorod; and Kirov, to mention just a few.

Most of society, even if not openly protesting, holds peoples from the North Caucasus in low esteem, refusing to see them as "Russians" and often limiting them to low-skilled, menial jobs such as farmer market traders in the major cities. Yet, the demographic dynamic suggests that the number of Russian citizens with Muslim roots is growing, and they occupy increasingly important socio-economic positions. For example, Rashid Nurgaliyev, who served as Russia's Interior Minister from 2003 to 2011, and Elvira Nabiullina, former Minister of Economic Development and Trade and current Head of Russian Central Bank, as well as many journalists, businesspeople, government officials, and law enforcement personnel. Putin, having to struggle with economic, political, and social problems throughout all of Russia, cannot risk having the North Caucasus reappear as a national crisis flashpoint, since it may lead to partial or even full loss of government control over the country. The Kremlin, therefore, has little choice but to continue its robust anti-terrorist policies with auxiliary economic and political support.

A favorable future in which the region prospers and Islamism becomes less appealing looks increasingly unlikely today. The outlook of the North Caucasus is bleak, and the possible scenarios range from a muddle through, more of the same/business as usual, including low intensity conflict, to a disastrous outcome in which the Russian state is unable to control the area, abandons the region, and Islamism takes a central role.

U.S. SECURITY INTERESTS AND THE
NORTH CAUCASUS CHALLENGES

In order to secure the best outcome for the region, the United States and its allies must continue to focus their attention on the North Caucasus. The following are the scenarios:

1. A significant improvement in socio-economic and political dynamics if there is a drop in terrorist recruitment and activity. This should decrease the need for governmental counterterrorist operations against the enemy and create a positive climate for investment;

2. A status quo, as the region continues its reliance on Moscow for subsidies, legitimacy, and support. The status quo would also continue to stigmatize the North Caucasus Muslims as citizens of lesser stature; in short, a muddle through;

3. Russian and local authorities' failures to maintain the order in the region, and the North Caucasus descends into chaos.

The status quo/muddle through remains the most likely long-term outcome for the region, unless Ramzan Kadyrov is killed or incapacitated; however, maintaining the status quo only makes the crisis more likely in the long term, since any significant economic deterioration may bring patience and acquiescence among the population to an end.

In light of the current situation, the United States must act to protect its interests in the American homeland, as well as in Europe, the Caucasus, the Middle East, and Central Asia. The United States must be committed to curbing the growth of Islamist terrorism and radicalism in the North Caucasus. The United States must engage its allies and work with Russia to strengthen its border security, invigorate law enforcement, and counterterrorist cooperation with national and international agencies, improve intelligence capabilities, and appeal for international cooperation to eliminate the financial support of terrorism that helps North-Caucasus militant groups flourish.

Without immediate, thorough, and concerted international action, the challenges that the North Caucasus presents to the world will grow into major problems. As the terrorist threat grows in the North Caucasus, the United States needs to improve the capabilities of the agencies most engaged in fighting it. Specifically, the United States can work with Georgia and Azerbaijan to improve their border security with Russia. The inability to track and to stop those who illegally cross the porous borders poses a great risk to the energy infrastructure in the South Caucasus. Engaging with Russia as well as American friends and allies in the region to prevent infrastructure attacks, as well as the smuggling of human beings, drugs and arms, would greatly help to protect the region from terrorism.

The United States may also help train and build relationships with intelligence, counterterrorist, and law enforcement agencies in South Caucasus, including Georgia, Azerbaijan, and Armenia. The United States can explore expanded cooperation with other foreign law enforcement and intelligence services for the collection of, prevention, and disruption of terrorist operations, including against American and friendly targets. U.S. intelligence and law enforcement agencies would benefit from cultivating regional ties and cooperating against such future threats as described in this monograph. Such cooperation will give the United States a better understanding of the North Caucasus threat from sources who know the languages, religions, cultures, history, and geography of the region.

The United States also needs to strive to uncover the North Caucasus terrorist networks that have connections to international terrorism. One effective way for the United States to stop North Caucasus-based terrorism is to hamper the means by which the groups grow and operate in the region and beyond. For example, this means that the United States should encourage Middle Eastern states to stop the transfer of funds to the North Caucasus extremists and cease their indoctrination and Salafi/Wahhabi education for global terrorist cadres, including recruiters and propagandists from the North Caucasus.

CONCLUSION

Over 2 centuries of abuses of the Russian imperial policy in the North Caucasus resonate even today. The North Caucasus has been a subject of the tsarist expansionist policies, communist oppression, Stalin's cruelty, and post-Soviet Russia's crippled and corrupt institutions, which, while providing some modernization drivers, sewed inter-ethnic and inter-religious discord and perpetuated the violent culture. The national reaction gave way to religious extremism. Russians did conquer the North Caucasus militarily, but they failed to assimilate the local population, extirpate the distinct identities of the North Caucasian peoples, or find a *modus vivendi* with Islam. The Chechens, the Ingush, the Circassians, and other local nations remember their tragic past and bear grudges against the Russians. Even though the Winter Olympics in Sochi in 2014 brought international attention to the tragedies of the region, fortunately, terrorist attacks never materialized during the games.

After two devastating wars at the end of the 20th century, Moscow has now largely rebuilt the destroyed Chechen infrastructure. On the surface, the Chechen capital Grozny looks more prosperous than ever. However, the Kremlin has failed to solve the underlying problems that fuel Islamist extremism and terrorism.

Improving the situation in the North Caucasus would ultimately require tackling corruption and ensuring government accountability to the local population—something that is highly unlikely to happen anytime soon. Soaring unemployment, unfair treatment of the North Caucasian ethnic minorities in Russia proper, the lack of opportunities, and a lack of belief in a better future motivate some of the Chechens, Ingush, Dagestanis, etc., to join violent groups active against the local governments and against Moscow — and in the cause of the global "holy war" against the "infidels."

The North Caucasus still faces a precarious future, as well as economic collapse and devastation. The growth of radical Islam and the danger of global jihad impeding on the region imperil not only Russia, but also the security of the U.S. homeland and allies. What was a nationalist struggle against Moscow has mutated over a short period of time into a global menace that already has spread to the Middle East, Central Asia, Europe, and the United States. The United States must track the threats from the North Caucasus and strive to prevent their further integration with global militant Islamist actors. Today, no American strategy against global Islamism will be effective without detailed programs and plans to combat terrorist networks in the North Caucasus.

ENDNOTES

1. Ariel Cohen, "A Threat to the West: The Rise of Islamist Insurgency in the Northern Caucasus and Russia's Inadequate Response," Heritage Foundation *Backgrounder*, No. 2643, March 26, 2012, available from *www.heritage.org/research/reports/2012/03/a-threat-to-the-west-the-rise-of-islamist-insurgency-in-the-northern-caucasus*.

2. "Designation of Caucasus Emirate," Washington, DC: U.S. Department of State, May 26, 2011, available from *www.state.gov/r/pa/prs/ps/2011/05/164312.htm*.

3. "Terakt v Kizlyare i Pervomayskom 9–18 yanvarya 1996 goda" ("A Terrorist Attack in Kizlyar and Pervomayskoye on January 9–January 18, 1996"), *Caucasian Knot*, January 18, 2013, available from *www.kavkaz-uzel.ru/articles/218853/*.

4. "Doku Umarov prikazal modzhakhedam ne atakovat grazhdanskoye naselenie Rossii" ("Doku Umarov Ordered the Mujahedeen not to Attack the Russian Civilian Population"), *Korrespondent.net*, February 3, 2012, available from *korrespondent. net/video/world/1315131-doku-umarov-prikazal-modzhahedam-ne-atakovat-grazhdanskoe-naselenie-rossii.*

5. "Greetings from Grozny: Explore Chechnya's Turbulent Past: 1700s: Holy War," PBS Wide Angle, July 25, 2002, available from *www.pbs.org/wnet/wideangle/episodes/greetings-from-grozny/explore-chechnyas-turbulent-past/1700s-holy-war/3304/.*

6. Leo Tolstoy, *Hadji Murat*, Chapter 12, 1917, available from *www.ccel.org/ccel/tolstoy/hadij.xiii.html.*

7. For more information on the background of the Russian/Soviet-North Caucasus conflicts, see Ariel Cohen, "A Threat to the West: The Rise of Islamist Insurgency in the Northern Caucasus and Russia's Inadequate Response," *Heritage Foundation Backgrounder* No. 2643, available from *www.heritage.org/research/reports/2012/03/a-threat-to-the-west-the-rise-of-islamist-insurgency-in-the-northern-caucasus.*

8. Paul B. Henze, "Islam in the North Caucasus: The Example of Chechnia," Santa Monica, CA: RAND Corporation, May 1995, p. 3, available from *www.circassianworld.com/pdf/Henze_Islam_NorthCaucasus.pdf.*

9. A. A. Alov and N. G. Vladimirov, "Rasprostranenie Islama sredi narodov Severnogo Kavkaza v VIII-XVIII vekax"/Islam v Rossii/Islam na Severnom Kavkaze, ("The Spread of Islam Among the Peoples of North Caucasus in the 'Eighth-Eighteenth Centuries' Islam in Russia/Islam in North Caucasus"), available from *www.verigi.ru/?book=200&chapter=27.*

10. "Ethnic Groups in the Caucasus Region," Washington, DC: Central Intelligence Agency, 1993.

11. Henze, p. 4.

12. Moshe Gammer, "'Proconsul of the Caucasus': A Re-examination of Yermolov," *Social Evolution & History*, Vol. 2, No. 1, March 2003, available from *www.sociostudies.org/journal/articles/140480/*.

13. E. A. Yermolov, "Zapiski (str. 20)" ("Notes (p. 20)"), available from *www.pandia.ru/text/77/390/36749-20.php*.

14. "Zhizn i deyatel'nost A. P. Yermolova" ("Life and Work of A. P. Yermolov"), 2006, available from *chechenasso.ru/?page_id=2163*.

15. I. Drozdov, "Poslednaya borba s gortsami na Zapad-nom Kavkaze" ("The Last Battle with the Highlanders in the Western Caucasus"), 1877, available from *www.vostlit.info/Texts/Dokumenty/Kavkaz/XIX/1840-1860/Drozdov_I/text3.htm*.

16. Vladimir Degoyev, "Imam Shamil (prorok, vlastitel, voin)," ("Imam Shamil [a Prophet, a Ruler, and a Warrior]"), 2001, p. 131.

17. Vladimir Degoyev, "Imam Shamil i tekhnologiya vlastvovaniya" ("Imam Shamil and the Method of Ruling"), 1998, available from *www.russia-21.ru/xxi/rus_21/ARXIV/1998/degoev_7-8_98.htm*.

18. "Ichkeriyskoye srazhenie" ("The Ichkerinsky Battle"), *Caucasian Knot*, February 15, 2011.

19. G. G. Lisicyna, "Vospominaniya neizvestnogo uchast-nika Darginskoy ekspeditsii 1845 g." ("Memoirs of an Unknown Participant of the Dargo Expedition"), *Journal "Zvezda"* ("Star"), No. 6, 1996, pp. 181-191, available from *www.vostlit.info/Texts/Dokumenty/Kavkaz/XIX/1840-1860/Neizv_uc_darg_exp/text1.htm*.

20. N. N. Velikaya, "Kazaki Vostochnogo Predkavkazya v XVIII-XIX VV" ("Cossacks of Eastern Ciscaucasia in the 17th-19th Centuries"), 2001, available from *www.cossackdom.com/book/bookkazak2.html*.

21. Svante E. Cornell, "The 'Afghanization' of the North Caucasus: Causes and Implications of a Changing Conflict," *Rus-*

sia's Homegrown Insurgency: Jihad in the North Caucasus, Carlisle, PA: Strategic Studies Institute, U.S. Army War College. October 2012, p. 125.

22. Z. Papaskiri, "Nekotoryye aspekty imperskoy politiki Rossii na Kavkaze" ("Some Aspects of the Russian Imperial Policy in the Caucasus"), July 11, 2012, available from *rus.expert-club.ge/portal/cnid__12208/alias__Expertclub/lang__ru/tabid__2546/default.aspx*.

23. Drozdov, "The Last Battle with the Highlanders in the Western Caucasus."

24. Henze, p. 4.

25. "Istoricheskiy obzor: tragediya adygov v Kavkazskoy voyne" ("A Historical Review: the Tragedy of the Circassians in the Caucasian War"), May 25, 2013, available from *history-tema. com/istoricheskij-obzor-tragediya-adygov-v-kavkazskoj-vojne*.

26. *Ibid.*

27. S. M. Dmitrievskiy, B. I. Gvareli, O. A. Chelysheva, "Mezhdunarodnyy Tribunal Dlya Chechni" ("An International Tribunal for Chechnya"), Nizhniy Novgorod, Russia, 2009, p. 68, available from *old.novayagazeta.ru/file/pdf/t1.pdf*.

28. D. Gakaev, "Grazhdanskaya voyna v Checheno-Ingushetii"/Ocherki politicheskoy istorii Chechni (XX vek) ("The Civil War in Checheno-Ingushetia"/Essays on the Political History of Chechnya (20th Century)), available from *checheninfo.ru/12438-grazhdanskaya-voyna-v-checheno-ingushetii.html*.

29. Victor A. Shnirelman, "Byt Alanami: intellektualy i politika na Severnom Kavkaze v XX veke" ("To Be Alans: Intellectuals and Politics in the North Caucasus in the 20th Century"), 2006, p. 38, available from *old.ingushetiyaru.org/history/shnirelman_bit_alanamy/files/shnirelman_bit_alanamy.doc*.

30. Yu. V. Yeremina, "Otechestvennaya istoriya. Uchebno-prakticheskoye posobiye dlya studentov vsekh spetsialnostey i vsekh form obucheniya" ("Domestic History. Educational and

Practical Handbook for Students of all Specializations and all Forms of Training"), General-purpose textbook for students, Part 2, Moscow, Russia: Moscow State University of Economics, Statistics and Computer Science, 2010, pp. 9–10, available from *www.bytic.ru/mesi/Zadanie/%D0%9E%D1%82%D0%B5%D1%87 %D0%B5%D1%81%D1%82%D0%B2%D0%B5%D0%BD%D0% BD%D0%B0%D1%8F%20%D0%B8%D1%81%D1%82%D0%BE %D1%80%D0%B8%D1%8F/%D0%9E%D1%82%D0%B5%D1%8 7.%D0%B8%D1%81%D1%82%D0%BE%D1%80%D0%B8%D1% 8F%202.doc.*

31. "Deklaraciya prav narodov Rossii, 2(15) noyabrya 1917 g." ("Declaration of the Rights of the Peoples of Russia, November 2(15), 1917"), Decrees of the Soviet Authorities, 1957, available from *www.hist.msu.ru/ER/Etext/DEKRET/peoples.htm.*

32. Cohen, p. 5.

33. "Remembering Stalin's Deportations," *BBCNews*, February 23, 2004, available from *news.bbc.co.uk/2/hi/3509933.stm.*

34. "Dokumenty iz arkhiva Iosifa Stalina" ("Documents from the Archive of Joseph Stalin"), *Novaya Gazeta*, February 29, 2000, available from *www.ng.ru/specfile/2000-02-29/10_top_secret.html.*

35. N. F. Bugay, "Pravda o deportacii chechenskogo i ingushs-kogo narodov" ("The Truth about the Deportation of the Chechen and the Ingush Nations"), *Voprosy istorii (Historical Issues)*, No. 7, 1990, available from *www.ingush.ru/repressii4.asp.*

36. "Ukaz ot 12 oktyabrya 1943 goda O likvidacii Karachae-vskoy Avtonomnoy Oblasti i ob administrativnom ustrojstve yeyo territorii" ("Decree of October 12, 1943, on the Liquidation of the Karachevo Autonomous Oblast and about the Administrative Organization of its Territory"), available from *www.libussr.ru/doc_ussr/ussr_4462.htm.*

37. "Ukaz Prezidiuma Verkhovnogo Soveta SSSR O likvida-cii Kalmyckoy ASSR i obrazovanii Astraxanskoy oblasti v sostave RSFSR" ("Decree of the Supreme Soviet of the USSR On the Liquidation of the Kalmyk ASSR and the Creation of the Astrahkans-kaya Oblast as part of the RSFSR"), available from *www.memorial. krsk.ru/DOKUMENT/USSR/431227.htm.*

38. "Deportaciya narodov v SSSR. Spravka" ("Deportation of the Peoples of the USSR. Overview"), *RIA Novosti*, November 14, 2009, available from *ria.ru/society/20091114/193419498.html*.

39. Alexander Janda, Nobert Leitner, and Mathias Vogl, *Chechens in the European Union*, Vienna, Austria: Austrian Integration Fund, 2008, p. 13.

40. Zeyno Baran, S. Frederick Starr, and Svante E. Cornell, "Islamic Radicalism in Central Asia and the Caucasus: Implications for the EU," *Central Asia-Caucasus Institute Silk Road Studies*, July 2006, available from *www.silkroadstudies.org/new/docs/Silkroadpapers/0607Islam.pdf*.

41. Cornell, p. 127.

42. See Vakhit Akaev, "The History and Specifics of the Islamic Renaissance Today in the Chechen Republic," *Central Asia and the Caucasus*, Vol. 12, Issue 3, 2011, pp. 97-102.

43. See Ianda *et al.*, p. 31.

44. The ASSRs consisted of Chechen-Ingush ASSR, Dagestan ASSR, North Ossetian ASSR, Karbardino-Balkar ASSR, Karachai-Cherkess ASSR, and Adigeian ASSR. These ASSRs became Autonomous Republics of the Russian Federation. (The Chechen-Inguish ASSR split in two along ethnic lines.)

45. Henry Sokolski, "Beyond Nunn-Lugar: Curbing the Next Wave of Weapons Proliferation Threats from Russia," Washington, DC: Nonproliferation Policy Education Center, April 2002, p. 65.

46. A. V. Cherkasov and O. P. Orlov, "Khronika vooruzhennogo konflikta" ("A Chronicle of the Armed Conflict"), *Memorial*, available from *www.memo.ru/hr/hotpoints/chechen/itogi/xp90.htm*.

47. Cohen, p. 5.

48. Cornell, pp. 128-129.

49. See "Agreement between the Government of the Russian Federation and the Government of the Republic of Tatarstan," Kazan, Tatarstan: Kazan State University, May 20, 2013. See also "Relations Between the Federal Centre and Tatarstan," available from *1997-2011.tatarstan.ru/?DNSID=835e288e889a320f22475f56cf 81d5f1&node_id=836.*

50. "Naselenie po natsionalnosti i vladeniyu russkim ya-zykom po subyektam Rossiyskoy Federatsii" (The Population of the Russian Federation in Territorial Units by Nationality and Russian Language Fluency), available from *www.perepis2002.ru/ ct/doc/TOM_04_03.xls.*

51. V. Zaytsev, "Nayomniki v Chechne" ("Mercenaries in Chechnya"), *Journal "Ogonyok"* ("Little Fire"), No. 11, 5170, March 21, 2011, available from *www.kommersant.ru/doc/1604045.*

52. "Posledneye intervyu Pavla Grachova: 'Po Belomu domu, beglymi, ogon!'" ("The Last Interview of Pavel Grachev: 'Running Fire at the White House!'"), *Forbes*, October 16, 2012, available from *www.forbes.ru/sobytiya/lyudi/167386-poslednee-intervyu-pavla-gracheva-po-belomu-domu-beglymi-ogon?page=0,1.*

53. Svante E. Cornell, "The 'Afghanization' of the North Caucasus," Stephen J. Blank, ed., *Russia's Homegrown Insurgency: Jihad in the North Caucasus*, Carlisle, PA: Strategic Studies Institute, U.S. Army War College, 2012, p. 127.

54. Ilyas Akhmadov and Miriam Lanskoy, *The Chechen Struggle: Independence Won and Lost*, New York: Palgrave MacMillan, 2010, p. 12.

55. *Ibid.*, pp. 12-13.

56. *Ibid.*

57. "Vzyat' Groznyy silami odnogo parashyutno-desant-nogo polka" ("To Capture Grozny with One Airborne Regiment"), *RIA Novosti*, April 17, 2011, available from *ria.ru/history_ tochki/20110417/365652355.html.*

58. Cornell, p. 130.

59. *Ibid.*

60. *Ibid.*

61. David Zucchino, "Chechen Commando Chief Recounts Budyonnovsk Raid, Events that Preceded It," *Knight-Ridder News Service,* July 16, 1995, available from *articles.baltimoresun.com/1995-07-16/news/1995197017_1_basayev-budyonnovsk-chechen-war.*

62. "Khronologiya zakhvata zalozhnikov v gorode Budyonnovsk. Spravka" ("A Chronology of the Hostage Taking in the Town of Budyonnovsk: Overview"), *RIA Novosti,* June 11, 2011, available from *ria.ru/history_spravki/20110610/386717117.html.*

63. "Budyonnovsk, June 1995, Chronicles of a Deadly Terrorist Attack," *RIA Novosti,* No Date, available from *en.rian.ru/photolents/20100618/159475084_12.html.*

64. Cornell, p. 131.

65. "Zakhvaty zalozhnikov. Kak eto bylo v mire" ("Hostage Taking: How It Was in the World"), *Izvestiya,* October 24, 2002, available from *izvestia.ru/news/268869.*

66. "Snayperskaya voyna v Chechne" ("Sniper War in Chechnya"), available from *www.bratishka.ru/zal/sniper/3_7.php.*

67. O. Lukin, "Pervaya chechenskaya voyna: Mif o 'malenkoy pobedonosnoy voyne' rasseivaetsya" ("The First Chechen War: The Myth about the 'Short Victorious War' Is Dissipating"), *Journal "Mostok"* ("Little Bridge"), March–June 1995, available from *www.vestnikmostok.ru/index.php?categoryid=19&view=arhiv&view_num=19&id_item=118&action=view.*

68. E. A. Fedosov, "Polveka v aviatsii: Zapiski akademika," ("Half a Century in Aviation: Notes of an Academic"), Moscow, Russia, 2004, available from *militera.lib.ru/memo/russian/fedosov_ea/05.html.*

69. "Organizatsii, svyazannye s Al-Kaidoy" ("Organizations Linked to Al Qaeda"), September 3, 2010, available from *www.un.org/russian/sc/committees/1267/NSQE9903R.shtml.*

70. Arkady Babchenko, "Uncivil War," *The Washington Post*, March 30, 2008, available from *www.washingtonpost.com/wp-dyn/content/article/2008/03/27/AR2008032702932_pf.html*.

71. Arthur L. Speyer III, "The Two Sides of Grozny," Santa Monica, CA: The RAND Corporation, available from *www.rand.org/content/dam/rand/pubs/conf_proceedings/CF162/CF162.appc.pdf*.

72. *Ibid.*, p. 71.

73. *Ibid.*, p. 90.

74. *Ibid.*, p. 70.

75. D. Ivanov, "Aslan Maskhadov proigral voynu" ("Aslan Maskhadov Lost the War"), *Lenta.Ru*, March 9, 2005, available from *lenta.ru/articles/2005/03/08/maskhadov/*.

76. I. Yegorov, "Al-Kaida v Rossii" ("Al Qaeda in Russia"), *Rossiyskaya Gazeta*, May 2, 2011, available from *www.rg.ru/2011/05/02/alkaida-site.html*.

77. *Ibid.*

78. Lev Gudkov, "Pokornoe bessilie rossiyskogo obshchestva" ("Obedient Powerlessness of the Russian Society"), *BBC*, December 1, 2004, available from *news.bbc.co.uk/hi/russian/russia/newsid_4059000/4059361.stm*.

79. "Pervaya Chechenskaya voyna 1994-1996" ("The First Chechen War of 1994–1996"), December 12, 2009, available from *history-of-wars.ru/war_hrono/343-pervaya-chechenskaya-vojna-1994-1996.html*.

80. Alexei Malashenko and Dmitri Trenin, "Vremya yuga. Rossiya v Chechne, Chechnya v Rossii" ("The Time of the South: Russia in Chechnya and Chechnya in Russia"), Moscow, Russia, 2002, pp. 47-48, available from *carnegieendowment.org/files/pub-35864.pdf*.

81. *Ibid.*

82. "Chechnya i Sostoyaniye Rossiyskoy Armii" ("Chechnya and the State of the Russian Military"), 2001, available from *www. mfit.ru/defensive/vestnik/vestnik6_1.html*.

83. S. E. Miller and Dmitri Trenin, "Vooruzhonnye sily Rossii: vlast i politika" ("Russia's Armed Forces: Power and Politics"), Cambridge, MA: MIT Press, 2005, p. 61, available from *www. amacad.org/publications/russian_mil_russian.pdf*.

84. Liz Fuller, "Why Is The North Caucasus An Unholy Mess?" *Radio Free Europe*, July 11, 2013, available from *www.rferl.org/content/north_caucasus_why_is_it_such_an_unholy_mess/24297384. html*.

85. Alexei Kudryavtsev, "Vakhabbism": problemy religioznogo ehkstremizma na Severnom Kavkaze" ("'Wahhabism': Problems with Religious Extremism in the North Caucasus"), Lulea, Sweden: Central Asian and Central Caucasus (CA&CC) Press, September 2000, available from *www.ca-c.org/journal/cac-09-2000/14.Kudriav.shtml*.

86. Ilya Maksakov, "Shariatskoye pravo po-chechenski" ("Sharia Law in Chechen"), *Nezavisimaya Gazeta*, February 29, 2000, available from *www.ng.ru/specfile/2000-02-29/14_shariat.html*.

87. Leon Aron, "Chechnya. New Dimensions of the Old Crisis," Washington, DC: American Enterprise Institute, February 1, 2003, available from *www.aei.org/article/foreign-and-defense-policy/regional/europe/chechnya-outlook/#mbl*.

88. Cohen, p. 5.

89. "Ekonomika chechenskogo terrora" ("Economics of the Chechen Terror"), *Kommersant*, No. 36, 240, September 15, 1999, available from *www.kommersant.ru/doc/23319/*.

90. A. K. Bekryashev, I. P. Belozerov, and N. S. Bekryasheva, "Tenevaya ekonomika i ekonomicheskaya prestupnost" ("The Shadow Economy and Economic Crime"), 2003, p. 207, available from *rrc.dgu.ru/res/economika/ten_ec.doc*.

91. Akhmadov *et al.*, pp. 123-124.

92. Cornell, p. 133.

93. *Ibid.*, p. 133-134.

94. Sanobar Shermatova and Leonid Nikitinsky, "Generaly rabotorgovli" ("The Generals of the Slave Trade"), *Moskovskiye Novosti*, March–April 2000, available from *www.memo.ru/hr/ hotpoints/N-Caucas/ch99/000328/mn0328a.htm*.

95. Vladimir Ardaev, "Kem byl Arbi Barayev" ("Who Was Arbi Barayev"), *BBC*, June 25, 2001, available from *news.bbc.co.uk/ hi/russian/news/newsid_1407000/1407433.stm*.

96. Gennadiy Troshev, "Moya voyna. Chechenskiy dnevnik okopnogo generala" ("My War. The Chechen Diary of a Trench General"), 2001, available from *www.lib.ru/MEMUARY/ CHECHNYA/troshew.txt_with-big-pictures.html*.

97. "Chistoserdechnoye Priznanie—Kavkazskiye Plenniki" ("Open-Hearted Confession—Caucasian Captives"), NTV, 2005, available from *www.youtube.com/watch?v=4QKyOwPeNa8*.

98. Timur Aliyev, "Chechnya: biznes na voyne" ("Chechnya: the War Business"), BBC, December 10, 2004, available from *news. bbc.co.uk/hi/russian/russia/newsid_4044000/4044675.stm*.

99. "Open-Hearted Confession—Caucasian Captives."

100. *Ibid.*

101. Cornell, p. 135.

102. Akhmadov, pp. 173-176.

103. Cornell, p. 138.

104. Cohen, p. 5.

105. Alexander Cherkasov, "Demografiya, poteri naseleniya i migracionnye potoki v zone vooruzhonnogo konflikta v Chechenskoy Respublike. Kritika istochnikov" ("The Book of Numbers, Demographics, Civilian Losses and Migration Flows in the Conflict Zone in the Republic of Chechnya: A Critique of

the Sources"), Stavropol, Russia: *Kniga chisel*, *Memorial*, September 2001, available from *www.memo.ru/hr/hotpoints/N-Caucas/misc/numbook.htm*.

106. *U.S. Department of State Country Report on Human Rights Practices 1996-Russia*, Washington, DC: United States Department of State, January 30, 1997, available from *www.refworld.org/docid/3ae6aa7b0.html*.

107. Maria Mstislavskaya, "Vysshaya chechenskaya arifmetika" ("Higher Chechen Arithmetic"), *Lenta.Ru*, August 16, 2005, available from *lenta.ru/articles/2005/08/16/losses/*.

108. "Kak okhotilis na Akhmata Kadyrova" ("How Akhmat Kadyrov Was Hunted"), *Kommersant*, May 11, 2004, available from *www.kommersant.ru/doc/473143*.

109. D. Ivanov, "Aslan Maskhadov proigral voynu" ("Aslan Maskhadov Lost the War"), *Lenta.Ru*, March 9, 2005, available from *lenta.ru/articles/2005/03/08/maskhadov/*.

110. "Sledstvie: Maskhadova zastrelil okhrannik" ("Investigation: Maskhadov Was Shot Dead by his Bodyguard"), *Agentura. Ru*, October 28, 2005, available from *www.agentura.ru/news/21800/*.

111. "Shamaev Akhmad-khadzhi," October 17, 2000, available from *www.religio.ru/dosje/24/63.html*.

112. "Osuzhdyonnyye za ubiystvo Yandarbiyeva vernulis v Rossiyu" ("Those Sentenced for Killing Yandarbiyev Returned to Russia"), *Rossiyskaya Gazeta*, December 23, 2004, available from *www.rg.ru/2004/12/24/katar-anons.html*.

113. "Russian Justice Ministry Knows, Yandarbiyev's Killers Serve Sentence in Russia, Doesn't Know Where," *Regnum*, December 14, 2005, available from *www.regnum.ru/english/560154.html*.

114. Interview with Sergey Markedonov, Visiting Fellow, Washington, DC: Center for Strategic and International Studies (CSIS), July 20-24, 2013.

115. Ildar Bedretdinov, "Vtoraya Chechenskaya voyna" ("The Second Chechen War"), 2004, available from *www.airwar.ru/ history/locwar/chechnya/sw/sw.html*.

116. "Kavkaz: Vtoraya chechenskaya vojna" ("The Caucasus: the Second Chechen War"), 2000, available from *razumkov.org.ua/ ukr/article.php?news_id=565*.

117. "PVO i poteri udarnykh vertolyotov" ("Air Defense Systems and Losses of Attack Helicopters"), *Newsland.com*, January 15, 2013, available from *newsland.com/news/detail/id/1106730/*.

118. *Ibid.*

119. "Na Argunskoe ushhelye sbrasyvayut obyomno-detoniruyushhiye bomby" ("Thermobaric Weapons are Being Thrown Down on the Argun Gorge"), *Lenta.Ru*, February 9, 2000, available from *lenta.ru/vojna/2000/02/09/argun/*.

120. Lester W. Grau and Timothy Smith, "A 'Crushing' Victory: Fuel-Air Explosives and Grozny 2000," August 2000, available from *fmso.leavenworth.army.mil/documents/fuelair/fuelair.htm*.

121. Gordon M. Hahn, "Caucasus Emirate Jihadists: The Security and Strategic Implications," Stephen J. Blank, ed., *Russia's Homegrown Insurgency: Jihad in the North Caucasus,* Carlisle, PA: Strategic Studies Institute, U.S. Army War College, October, 2012, p. 29, available from *www.strategicstudiesinstitute.army.mil/pdffiles/ PUB1116.pdf*.

122. Liz Fuller, "Chechnya: Resistance Leadership Affirms Readiness for Peace Talks," RFE/RL, July 14, 2006, available from *www.rferl.org/content/article/1069862.html*.

123. Gordon Hahn, "The Caucasus Emirate Jihadists," Stephen J. Blank, ed., *Russia's Homegrown Insurgency: Jihad in the North Caucasus,* Carlisle, PA: Strategic Studies Institute, U.S. Army War College, October, 2012, p. 3. (The *Jamaat* reference comes from Cohen, "A Threat to the West," p. 7.)

124. *Ibid.*, pp. 5-6.

125. *Ibid.*, p. 7.

126. Cohen, p. 6.

127. Hahn,"Amir Doku Abu Usman o bin Ladene, Imarate Kavkaz I poteryakh modzhakhedov" ("Amir Doku Abu Usman on bin Laden, the Caucasus Emirate and Losses of the Mujahedeen"), *Kavkaz tsentr*, May 17, 2011, p. 10, available from *www. kavkazcenter.com/russ/content/2011/05/17/81607.shtml.*

128. Cohen, p. 7.

129. From Cohen, "Top Al Qaeda Envoy Killed in Chechnya," *RT*, May 4, 2011, available from *rt.com/news/qaeda-terrorism-killed-chechnya/.*

130. From Cohen, p. 7, Rachel Ehrenfeld and Jonathan Halevi, "Al Qaeda's Global Reach," New York: American Center for Democracy, May 12, 2010, available from *acdemocracy.org/Al Qaedas-global-reach/.*

131. "ESPCh: operatsiya na Dubrovke byla provedena s narusheniyami" ("The Operation in Dubrovka Was Conducted with Violations"), *BBC Russian*, December 20, 2011, available from *www.bbc.co.uk/russian/russia/2011/12/111220_strasbourg_court_nord-ost.shtml.*

132. "Nord-Ost. Neokonchennoye rassledovanie" — doklad pod takim nazvaniem predstavili segodnya obshhestvennosti rodstvenniki pogibshikh i postradavshiye pri terakte na Dubrovke." ("Nord-Ost. An Unfinished Investigation — A Report under this Name Was Released Today by Relatives of the Victims and by Those Injured"), *Ekho Moskvy*, May 15, 2006, available from *www. echo.msk.ru/news/322802.html.*

133. "Minzdrav oyavil sostav gaza iz "Nord-Osta" gosudarstvennoy taynoy" ("The Ministry of Health Has Declared the Composition of the Gas Used in Nord-Ost a Government Secret"), *Lenta.Ru*, December 11, 2002, available from *lenta.ru/terror/2002/12/11/gas/.*

134. "Veteran Alfy: primeneniye gaza pri shturme "Nord-Os-ta" bylo opravdano" ("An Alpha Veteran: Using Gas at Freeing Nord-Ost Was Justified"), *RIA Novosti*, October 26, 2012, available from *ria.ru/society/20121026/906935884.html*.

135. "Sentyabrskiye vzryvy 1999 goda" ("September 1999 Blasts"), *RIA Novosti*, September 12, 2011, available from *ria.ru/history_comments/20110912/436010306.html*.

136. From Cohen, p. 6, "QI.U.190.11. Doku Khamatovich Umarov," New York: UN Security Council, March 10, 2011, available from *www.un.org/sc/committees/1267/NSQI29011E.shtml*; "Designation of Caucasus Emirate Leader Doku Umarov," Washington, DC: U.S. Department of State, 2010; "Designation of Caucasus Emirate," Washington, DC: US Department of State, 2011.

137. "Khronika zakhvata zalozhnikov v shkole nomer 1 g. Beslan. Spravka" ("A Chronicle of the Hostage Taking in School No. 1 in Breslan: Overview"), *RIA Novosti*, September 1, 2009, available from *ria.ru/society/20090901/183228293.html*.

138. Roman Osharov, "'Golos Beslana': Narod pomnit. . . . A vlasti?" (Roman Osharov, "'The Voice of Beslan:' The People Remember. . . . And the Authorities?"), *Voice of America*, September 3, 2012, available from *www.golos-ameriki.ru/content/beslan-russia/1500567.html*.

139. "Doklad komissii Torshina razocharoval 'Materey Beslana'" ("The Report of the Torshin Commission Has Disappointed the 'Mothers of Beslan'"), *Lenta.Ru*, December 28, 2005, available from *lenta.ru/news/2005/12/28/beslan1/*.

140. Fedor Maksimov, "Beslan obyasnili vzryvtexticheski" ("Beslan Explained through Blasts"), *Kommersant*, September 4, 2006, available from *www.kommersant.ru/doc/702175/*.

141. From Cohen, p. 6, National Consortium for the Study of Terrorism and Responses to Terrorism, "Suicide Attack at Moscow Airport," *Background Report,* January 24, 2011, available from *www.start.umd.edu/start/publications/br/Background_Report_2011_January_Moscow_Airport.pdf*.

142. Meeting with Vladimir Putin, Valday Club, Moscow, Russia, September 2004 (author's notes).

143. Sergey Markedonov, personal interview, July 23, 2013.

144. *Ibid.*

145. "Adhmad Kadyrov's Death Marked the End of an Era," *RIA Novosti*, May 13, 2005, available from *en.rian.ru/analysis/20050513/39977649.html*.

146. C. J. Chivers, "Investigation Links Critic's Death to Top Chechens," *The New York Times*, April 25, 2010, available from *www.nytimes.com/2010/04/26/world/europe/26chechen.html?pagewanted=all&_r=0*.

147. Anatol Lieven, "Gracious Grozny," *The National Interest*, September 18, 2008, available from *nationalinterest.org/article/gracious-grozny-2865*.

148. Tom Parfitt, "The Battle for the Soul of Chechnya," *The Guardian*, November 22, 2007, available from *www.guardian.co.uk/world/2007/nov/22/chechnya.tomparfitt*.

149. Cohen, p. 8.

150. Parfitt.

151. Mairbek Vatchagaev, "Large-Scale Clash with Insurgents Reported in Chechnya in Bamut," *Jamestown Foundation*, July 11, 2013, available from *www.jamestown.org/regions/thecaucasus/single/?tx_ttnews[tt_news]=41110&tx_ttnews[backPid]=639&cHash=0f6f9cca3d2d62e7b7af0d435ed9dd3d#.Ueyk5W008mU*.

152. Alexei Malashenko, personal interview, July 20, 2013.

153. *Ibid.*

154. "U.S. Congress: Russia Uses Terrorist Tactics in Caucasus," *Kavkaz Center*, April 24, 2011, available from *www.kavkazcenter.com/eng/content/2011/04/24/14158.shtml*.

155. "The Committee of the USA for International Religious Freedoms Advises the USA to Block Ramzan Kadyrov's Bank Accounts," *Caucasian Knot,* May 5, 2011, available from *eng. kavkaz-uzel.ru/articles/16966/.*

156. "Chechen Leader Kadyrov Laughs off Magnitsky List Rumors," *RIA Novosti*, April 13, 2013, available from *en.rian.ru/ russia/20130413/180621103.html.*

157. Vakhit Akaev,"The History and Specifics of the Islamic Renaissance Today in the Chechen Republic," *Central Asia and the Caucasus,* Vol. 12, Issue 3, 2011, Lulea, Sweden: CA&CC Press, pp. 97-104.

158. Akaev, pp. 101-102.

159. "Valovoy regionalnyy produkt po subyektam Rossiys-koy Federatsii na dushu naseleniya v 1998-2010" ("Gross Regional Product per Capita by Territorial Units of the Russian Federation in 1998–2010"), available from *www.gks.ru/free_doc/new_site/ vvp/dusha98-10.xls.*

160. "V 2012 godu v Chechenskoy Respublike nablyudalos snizhenie urovnya bezrabotitsy" ("Chechnya Saw a Decline in Unemployment in 2012"), January 11, 2013, available from *chechnya.gov.ru/page.php?r=126&id=12197.*

161. Anastasia Kirilenko, "Chechne neobxodimy investitsii ne tolko v stroitelstvo" ("Chechnya needs Investment not only in the Construction Sector"), *Caucasian Knot,* February 23, 2010, available from *www.kavkaz-uzel.ru/articles/165773/.*

162. Michael Schwirtz, "Russian Anger Grows Over Chechnya Subsidies," *The New York Times*, October 8, 2011, available from *www.nytimes.com/2011/10/09/world/europe/chechnyas-costs-stir-anger-as-russia-approaches-elections.html?pagewanted=all%20 2013,%20http:\ \www.nytimes.com\ \2011\ \10\ \09\ \world\ \ europe\ \chechnyas-costs-stir-anger-as-russia-approaches-elections. html%3fpagewanted=all".*

163. Mairbek Vatchagaev, "Continuing Human Rights Abuses Force Chechens to Flee to Europe," Washington, DC:

Jamestown Foundation, March 7, 2013, available from *www. jamestown.org/single/?no_cache=1&tx_ttnews[tt_news]=40559&tx_ ttnews[backPid]=623#.UdxnI231bYQ.*

164. Timur Malsagov, "Chechentsy po-evropeyski" ("Chechens in a European Way"), *Caucasus Times*, March 19, 2009, available from *www.caucasustimes.com/article.asp?id=19774.*

165. World Chechen Congress registration, 2005, available from *www.ejustice.just.fgov.be/tsv_pdf/2005/09/27/05134537.pdf.*

166. "Zayavleniye Chechenskaya Diaspora Norvegii," ("Statement of the Chechen Diaspora of Norway"), *Chechenews. com*, December 9, 2010, available from *chechenews.com/world-news/ breaking/1739-1.html.*

167. "Virtual 'World Chechen Congress' Was Staged," *Kavkazcenter.com*, September 26, 2010, available from *www. kavkazcenter.com/eng/content/2010/09/26/12582.shtml.*

168. *Ibid.*

169. Timur Malsagov, "Chechentsy po-evropeyski" ("Chechens in a European Way"), *Caucasus Times*, March 19, 2009, available from *www.caucasustimes.com/article.asp?id=19774.*

170. Hahn, pp. 47-49.

171. "Khishcheniya 275 mln rub vyyavleny v kompanii Kurorty Severnogo Kavkaza" ("Theft of 275 million Rubles in the Resorts of the North Caucasus Company Has Been Discovered"), *Argumenty i Fakty*, May 8, 2013, available from *www.aif.ru/money/ corruption/303920.*

172. Anastasia Bashkatova, "Korrupciya ustanovila olimpiyskiy rekord" ("Corruption Has Set an Olympic Record"), *Nezavisimaya Gazeta*, June 7, 2010, available from *www.ng.ru/economics/2010-06-07/1_corrupciya.html.*

173. Thomas Grove, "Special Report: Russia's $50 Billion Olympic Gamble," *Reuters*, February 21, 2013, available from *www.reuters.com/article/2013/02/21/us-russia-sochi-idUSBRE91K04M20130221.*

174. Maria Makutina, "Nemtsov ustanovil rekord Olimpiady" ("Nemtsov Set an Olympic Record"), *Gazeta.Ru*, May 30, 2005, available from *www.gazeta.ru/politics/2013/05/30_a_5362917.shtml*.

175. "Federalniy zakon Rossiyskoy Federatsii ot 6 marta 2006, No. 35-FZ O Protivodeistvii terrorizmu" ("Federal Law of the Russian Federation No. 35-FZ of March 6, 2006, On Combatting Terrorism"), *Rossiyskaya Gazeta*, March 10, 2006, available from *www.rg.ru/2006/03/10/borba-terrorizm.html*.

176. Murad Makhmudov and Lee Jay Walke, "Russian Federation: Doku Umarov: An Islamic Terrorist Vows to Stop Civilian Attacks," *Modern Tokyo Times*, February 18, 2012, available from *moderntokyotimes.com/2012/02/18/russian-federation-doku-umarov-an-islamic-terrorist-vows-to-stop-civilian-attacks/*; the quotes provided within the article are provided by Valery Dzutsev of the Jamestown Foundation.

177. Olga Gritsenko, "Terrorist v otstavke" ("A Retired Terrorist"), *Vzglyad.Ru*, August 2, 2010, available from *vzglyad.ru/politics/2010/8/2/422440.html*.

178. "Amir Imarata Kavkaz Doku Abu Usman otmenil svoyu otstavku, nazvav eyo sfabrikovannoy, i vystupil po etomu povodu so specialnym zayavleniyem" ("Doku(Abu Usman) Umarov, Emir of the Caucasus Emirate, Canceled his Resignation and Made a Special Statement on this Issue"), *Kavkaz Center*, August 4, 2010, available from *www.kavkazcenter.com/russ/content/2010/08/04/74303.shtml*.

179. Andrey Sharyy, "Andrey Babickiy — o Doku Umarove i vooruzhonnom podpolye" ("Andrey Babicky about Doku Umarov and the Armed Underground"), available from *www.svoboda.org/content/article/2000202.html*.

180. D. V. Makarov, "Nacionalnye otnosheniya. Radikalizaciya islama v Dagestane: Vozmozhnosti i predely dzhixadizma" ("Ethnic Relations. Radicalization of Islam in Dagestan: Possibilities and Limits of the Jihadism"), 2004.

181. Alexei Malashenko, "Kuda idyot Dagestan" ("Where Is Dagestan Going"), November 19, 2012, available from *carnegieendowment.org/2012/11/19/%D0%BA%D1%83%D0%B4%D0%B0-%D0%B8%D0%B4%D0%B5%D1%82-%D0%B4%D0%B0%D0%B3%D0%B5%D1%81%D1%82%D0%B0%D0%BD/elzq.*

182. Tanzila Chabieva and Michail Roshin, "Konflikt pokoleniy v ingushskom islame: sufii i salafity" ("A Conflict of Generations in Islam in Ingushetia: the Sufis and the Salafis"), *Caucasus Times*, April 29, 2013, available from *www.caucasustimes.com/article.asp?id=21140*.

183. "Konets 'rezhima antiterroristicheskoy operatsii' v Chechne" ("The End of 'Regime of Anti-Terrorism Operation' in Chechnya"), *RFI*, April 16, 2009, available from *www.rfi.fr/acturu/articles/112/article_3026.asp*.

184. Anton Krivenyuk, "Cherkesskiy mir mezhdu nacionalizmom i islamskoy globalizaciey" ("The Circassian World between Nationalism and Islamic Globalization"), *Caucasus Times*, May 2, 2013, available from *www.caucasustimes.com/article.asp?id=21144*.

185. "NAK: ubityye v Kabardino-Balkarii boeviki sobiralis sovershit terakty na Rozhdestvo" ("National Antiterrorist Committee: Rebels Killed in Kabardino-Balkaria Were Preparing to Commit Terrorist Attacks on Christmas"), *Caucasus Knot*, January 7, 2013, available from *www.kavkaz-uzel.ru/articles/218308/*.

186. "Kabardino-Balkariya: khronika vzryvov, obstrelov i teraktov" ("Kabardino-Balkaria: A Chronicle of Blasts, Firings, and Terrorist Attacks"), *Caucasus Knot*, originally published July 23, 2010, available from *kabardino-balkaria.kavkaz-uzel.ru/articles/172027/*.

187. Andrei Rezchikov and EkaterinaEermakova, "Chechenskiy sled doshol do Asada" ("The Chechen Trace Has Reached Assad"), *Vzglyad.Ru*, November 27, 2012, available from *vz.ru/politics/2012/11/27/609131.html*.

188. A. Malashenko, e-mail message to author, July 20, 2013.

189. Interview with Sergey Markedonov, Visiting Fellow, CSIS, July 20-24, 2013.

190. *Ibid.*

191. *Ibid.*

192. Olga Ivshina, "Radical Islam Raises Tension in Russia's Tatarstan," *BBC Russian*, August 8, 2012, available from *www.bbc.co.uk/news/world-europe-19179399*.

193. *Ibid.*

194. *Ibid.*

195. "Four Arrested in Anti-Terror Operation," *RT*, February 8, 2011, available from *rt.com/news/bashkortostan-terror-suspects-bomb/*.

196. Gordon M. Hahn, "Getting the Caucasus Emirate Right," Washington, DC: CSIS, August 2011, p. 4, available from *csis.org/files/publication/110930_Hahn_GettingCaucasusEmirateRt_Web.pdf*.

197. "Afghan Drug Traffic Aids Terrorists in North Caucasus—Drugs Official," *RIA Novosti*, June 9, 2010, available from *en.rian.ru/world/20100609/159354900.html*.

198. Hahn, "Getting the Caucasus Emirate Right," p. 5.

199. *Ibid.*

200. *Ibid.*, pp. 10-11.

201. Hahn, "The Caucasus-Emirate Jihadists," pp. 41-42.

202. Thomas Grove and Mariam Karouny, "Militants from Russia's North Caucasus Join Jihad in Syria," *Reuters*, March 6, 2013, available from *www.reuters.com/article/2013/03/06/us-syria-crisis-russia-militants-idUSBRE9251BT20130306*.

203. Interviews with government officials, Baku, Azerbaijan, May 2013, sources requested anonymity.

204. Marina Yegorova, "Moskvich o napadenii kavkaztsev: 'Mne rezali lob, ostavlyaya krovyanyye poloski, vtykali lezvie snachala v odnu nogu, potom v druguyu'" ("A Muscovite about Being Attacked by Caucasians: 'They cut my forehead, leaving blood stripes; they stuck a blade in one of my legs, then in the other one'"), *Komsomolskaya Pravda*, September 16, 2012, available from *www.kp.ru/daily/25950.5/2893267/*.

205. Nataliya Demidyuk, "V Saratovskoy oblasti mestnye zhiteli podralis s kavkaztsami" ("A Scuffle between the Locals and Caucasians in Saratovskaya Oblast"), *Moskovskiy Komsomolets*, July 8, 2013, available from *www.mk.ru/ incident/article/2013/07/08/880538-v-saratovskoy-oblasti-mestnyie-zhiteli-podralis-s-kavkaztsami.html*.